MOVIE WATCHER'S GUIDE TO
Enlightenment

David Hoffmeister

Movie Watcher's Guide to Enlightenment
by David Hoffmeister
ISBN: 978-0-9891000-2-1

Fourth Printed Edition 2013

Living Miracles Publications
P.O. Box 789, Kamas, UT 84036 USA
publishing@livingmiraclescenter.org
+1 435.200.4076

Living Miracles

This book was joyfully produced by the Living Miracles Community –
a non-profit ministry run by inspired mystics devoted to awakening.

David Hoffmeister

David Hoffmeister has touched the lives of thousands with his consistently peaceful state of mind, radiant joy and dedication to Truth. He is a modern-day mystic who has been invited to over 30 countries and 49 states to share the message of Love, Oneness and Freedom. His journey involved the study of many pathways culminating in a deeply committed practical application of *A Course in Miracles*. David's life is a living demonstration of the awakened mind. This is an invitation to join him.

For those who hope that enlightenment in this lifetime is possible, David is pure inspiration. His gentle demeanor and articulate non-compromising expression touches all who listen. His interest in practical application means the Answers are for everyone, resulting in widespread appeal. Using movies as modern-day parables David is as comfortable with young people delving into the metaphysics of *The Matrix* films as he is with those who have dedicated their lives to Buddhism, traditional Judeo-Christian religion as well as quantum physics. Basically anyone who has ever felt "there had to be a better way" or spontaneously burst into song, happy for no earthly reason, feels an affinity.

> Eventually everyone begins to recognize, however dimly,
> that there *must* be a better way. T-2.III.3.6

David is joined by the Living Miracles community which supports awakening through inspirational gatherings and retreats as well as a vast internet ministry. David has shared his insight on many spiritual talk shows and radio programs and freely offers in-depth teaching materials through audio/video and social media forums, allowing those with a deep call to connect from wherever they find themselves.

A Guide to Watching Movies

"Reel" Life?

What is real and what is illusion? Is watching a movie, being a character in a movie, or making a movie, any different than experiencing this world from a personal perspective? What constitutes acting and being an actor, as contrasted with being a *real person* in this seeming life? From the world's perspective there is a distinction made between ordinary life experience and the movies. With the Spirit's Vision, however, there is no such distinction. All is One.

With movies it is easy to watch the characters on the screen reflect your own dilemmas and need for acceptance, then after ninety minutes you get to watch them joyfully pop through in the miracle; it's a real time-saver/speed up. Why wait for drama to play out in your life when you can let the characters on the screen do it for you?

All feelings are based on interpretation of what seems to be on the screen, whether it is the screen of life or the silver screen. However, while in the comfort of your own home you can simply sit back and observe that everything is actually happening in *your mind*, allowing all feelings and emotions to come up for release.

The Basic Premise:

> All things I think I see reflect ideas. This is salvation's keynote:
> What I see reflects a process in my mind, which starts with my
> idea of what I want. From there, the mind makes up an image
> of the thing the mind desires, judges valuable, and therefore
> seeks to find. These images are then projected outward, looked
> upon, esteemed as real and guarded as one's own.
> (*A Course in Miracles*, W-325)

A Way of Looking

Investment in the drama versus detachment from it

Watching movies we practice stepping back and remembering that what we see on the screen is not real. In fact life itself is a big projection. What we see is not real but rather the out-picturing of our mind. Oh, but it is so easy to forget that! Watching movies in Purpose is a Way of Remembering.

How?

Come together with others, watch movies (images on the screen), and explore the feelings, thoughts and beliefs that surface. Discuss what has been uncovered through mind-watching during the movie (rather than judging the characters, the movie, the actors, the settings). In a state of sleep or mindlessness, perception is very unreliable; it changes continually. In a state of alertness or mindfulness, you are aware of and detached from "ego" thoughts and see everything and everyone differently. When the mind changes, perception changes, and the world you see is different from the way you saw it before.

Why?

For the Peace that comes with the stability of true perception. Ego thinking upholds the belief in separation by seeing victimization, competition and bodies. Ego confuses the mind about cause and effect; it distracts the mind from itself by drawing its attention to images on the screen. The Spirit's consistent Vision brings everything perceived on the screen back to the mind, where it can be seen as what it is – the mistaken out-picturing of the mind's false thoughts and beliefs.

The Spirit sees only wholeness, all things working together for good, and only two orders of thought: Love and a Call for Love.

Waking Up with the Movies

One

Be willing to stop the movie (pause your life) to detach from intense scenes, attractive scenarios, or moments when you want to know what will happen next. Watch the emotions and the investment in the images.

Two

Reread the Movie Guide synopsis frequently throughout to retrain the mind to see the symbols and characters of the movie as pointers to the Truth. It takes great mind training to consistently see the symbols as symbols and not to get lost in the drama.

Three

If you really want to go deep, use the *Instrument for Peace* worksheet (at the end of the book) to trace upsetting emotions back to the beliefs underneath them.

Four

Host a gathering. The Living Miracles community loves to work together to train the mind to see the movie of life differently and share the experience of deepening in an unfolding path to God. We invite people to enjoy our retreats and we also travel and share gatherings that incorporate these movie-watching techniques.

Themes

Listed below are some of the themes used to help you choose a movie for healing.

Mind-Watcher

Describes a movie that is used to flush up emotions in relation to a specific theme or to see how invested we can become in what is appearing on the screen. It can be helpful in what seems to be a safe context (i.e. watching a movie), to discover what our resistances and patterns are. Some of the movies have been identified as a mind-watcher as well as indicating what theme or emotion may be aroused. This can help the viewer to choose a movie that deals with a particular issue.

Metaphysical

This means beyond the physical or beyond the world and the world of bodies. Accurate metaphysics give a framework or reference point so that we can start to differentiate between the real and the unreal. We use this category to describe a movie that illustrates the metaphysics of *A Course in Miracles*. Movies like *The Matrix* or *Thirteenth Floor* are self-explanatory visual descriptions of these metaphysics. Movies like *Premonition*, with some interpretation or a good setup, can help bring to light false concepts of time.

Classic

The term classic describes those movies that inspire brotherhood and deep devotion, and can enjoyed repeatedly. These are helpful awakening movies that inspire and bless. We also use the term as "a classic for" a particular theme, such as unworthiness, for example, where the subject is very well addressed.

Awakening is Highly Individualized

Here are some movies that we have been intuitively drawn to on our inward journey. We are happy to share the insights which have been revealed by the Spirit within.

First there was *Brother Sun, Sister Moon*, and the Call to follow Christ was apparent. The Melody of the forgotten Song was stirred. Then followed *Groundhog Day* and the loop of time and the change of purpose needed for Escape was revealed.

Then there was *Dark City* and the underpinnings of a world of projection were exposed as the constructed false memories of misdirected mind – though when turned right side up, only Light, Love and Innocence remain as Reality. *The Truman Show* revealed what Shakespeare had foreshadowed: all the world's a stage, though Divine Mind must see it can play no "part." The contrived world of control and product placement was seen as a set and the show is effectively over when it is no longer believed as real. "Good afternoon, good evening, and good night" to illusions and dreams!

And then there was *The Matrix* – a composite of all that has been revealed in a parable of going entirely beyond the fabric of the dream to total Awakening – You are the One! Your mission, should you decide to accept it, is to Awaken immediately. The Way is set. This parable you know, a metaphysical masterpiece of the transcendence of belief.

Take the "red pill," follow the "white rabbit;" however it looks for you, answer the Call!

Love,
the Living Miracles
Community

All seemingly different paths to Truth converge and
are transcended in the Mystical Experience.

The experience ends the world of duality and
conflict forever and is one of clarity, of great joy,
and of deep peace and tranquility.

The experience is not of this world,
but radiates from within.

The Mystical Experience is not a concept, it comes
into awareness when all concepts have been laid by.

Forgiveness is the last concept there can be before
the Mystical Experience comes into awareness.

A Beautiful Mind (2001) – Mind-watcher for learning to discern and see unreal images as unreal

The sleeping mind sees people who are not really there and is paranoid about its safety and security. This love story is about the determination to reach equality and intimacy and transcend competition and fear, releasing false self-imposed limits. Though Love is ever-present, the necessity of healing and forgiveness is apparent for a beautiful mind willing to experience its Natural State of Mind. Faith Guides the mind beyond the maze of past associations to the Supreme Beauty of Love. The drive to succeed and achieve gives way to the only meaningful Prize: the awareness of Love.

Abyss, The (1989) – Metaphysical for going through the darkness to the light

The sleeping mind is like a deep, dark cavern in the ocean. The journey to the bottom of the abyss takes great faith. Along the way it often feels as if there will be no turning back from the darkness. But, when the mind is willing the means will be provided. To make it to the necessary depths the foreman of the oil rig has to use an apparatus that allows him to breathe liquid oxygen. To the ego the decision in mind for Total Trust is experienced as the anticipation of death, like the shock of the foreman's first intake of liquid into his lungs. Yet, with Trust and Purpose out front, the means are accepted, however frightening the shift in mind might feel, and the cliffs *can* be traversed. Ultimately in the depths of depths there awaits a realization that transcends all expectation, accompanied by angels of light. There is a Light that forever shines beyond the darkness in which communication is unbroken. This is the Light of Eternal Love!

Adam (2009) – Stepping out of fear and old patterns

Relationships are temporary assignments where an opportunity is offered to extend love and true empathy. With a willingness to train the mind and learn discernment, the Voice for God can be recognized and followed. Exposing thoughts may seem awkward and uncomfortable, but healing will occur swiftly when communication is open and honest. Saying what you mean and meaning what you say will open the door to true intimacy and connectedness.

"Feeling loved is very important, but loving…that's the necessity." When the lesson is learned, the relationship is no longer needed. In the end, the Spirit reveals that the love from another is no substitute for the love for another. Have the faith and courage to follow your heart and you will witness miracles!

Adjustment Bureau, The (2011) – Metaphysical, Power of thought

This is a world of doors. The Spirit can guide us through the use of these doors to return home. Doubt thoughts are always manifested. It is confusing, scary, and limiting to believe in an outer world that has power over you. The ego is always making adjustments to maintain its plan. When plans are given over to the Spirit, perception is adjusted; this is what leads to real fulfillment.

Holy encounters are the Spirit's substitute for the desires of this world. They provide a contrast experience that allows the mind to reach higher and higher to what it really wants. David Norris keeps running into his mighty companion, Elise. This fills the void that he tried to fill with the race for senator. It helps undo the belief that in order to fulfill his function he must sacrifice what his heart really wants.

Everyone is projecting onto the Chairman (God) what they believe. They are trying to understand and fulfill the Chairman's wishes as they perceive them. Yet even rules and structures that have served must ultimately be transcended for the even greater experience of Divine Love. Norris, in the end, decides to forgo all caution and opens the door of his heart, which leads directly to the Source. In his willingness to go for only love, all of the doubt thoughts disappear. Chance plays no part and sacrifice is never necessary; it is all a plan of the Spirit to awaken to one's True Identity beyond even the most glorified positions of this world. (Suggested reading: ACIM, Manual for Teachers, M-4.I.A, paragraphs 4 and 5).

AI: Artificial Intelligence (2001) – Mind-watcher for ego obscuring the truth

This is a futuristic story of Love that extends beyond biology, machines and technology. It illustrates a search for the Real Love that is in everyone's heart. In form, many issues arise that seem to obscure Eternal Love; abandonment and rejection are common feelings that block the Light. Yet Love prevails, and the witnesses to Love are beheld with the heart open and ready to receive.

Along Came Polly (2004) – Private thoughts, Holy relationship

No amount of planning can guarantee safety or a happy outcome in form. True happiness comes from forgiveness and opening to a present-moment love. Private thoughts and unhelpful beliefs can be released in the presence of the non-judgment of a true mighty companion; this is the basis of holy relationship. Love is letting go of fear and forgiving the need to protect a limited self-concept. Over and over again we see that when the moment comes to expose private thoughts, the threat was never what it seemed. Everything works together for good in the Spirit's plan. The present moment is all there is! Let My Love open the door!

Always (1989) Steven Spielberg – Undoing special relationship

The love we attempt to withhold is the only pain we carry. As we learn to help without wanting something in return, we remember the meaning of true love. Love does not possess. In helping and letting go of the desire to possess, we are Helped to understand unconditional love.

Always (1985) Henry Jaglom – Undoing special relationship

Letting go of expectations and control is the only way we experience a "happy ending." Living in the moment, free of the past, is the only state of mind in which we are in union and beyond the possibility of "divorce." True Union is Eternal, beyond the body and the world.

Amanda and the Alien (1995) TV Movie – Letting go of specialness and body identity

True love is extending and helping regardless of changing appearances. Form seems to shift and change, but love has its strength in the mind, and this love is fearless. Be not concerned about the form of the person you are with, for you are always with your Self. And when you help anyone, you are Helped.

American Beauty (1999) – Mind-watcher for transformation, Stepping out of the box, Undoing abuse ideas and family concepts

Let me accept all things exactly as they are. In a world of oddities and temptations, where everything seems to shift and change and distortions prevail, there is a peaceful Perspective that simply Observes in Peace.

Where judgments were, there remains a blessing which has been untouched. All things work together for good, and in this sacred Holy Instant a plastic bag dancing and swirling in the wind is beheld from the Point of Beauty. Glory to the Spirit Which is All Beauty and Perceives the Beauty of the whole and complete tapestry of the cosmos. Such is forgiveness.

Angel-A (2005)

Andre is compromising in many areas of his life. He attempts to act grandiose but the reflections he gets everywhere is that he is small and weak. But he is ready nonetheless. And when the mind is ready to awaken, just the right kind of angel will be sent to help you break through the boundaries of your personal world. Enter Angela.... Spirit always meets us where we think we are and graciously offers many opportunities to wash away any traces of guilt in the most inspiring way.

Anger Management (2003) – Repression, Fear of expressing emotions

Denial and repression can seem to keep pent-up anger from being expressed, but the time comes when it is important to take the lid off. A counseling relationship can be a backdrop to get in touch with unconscious anger and begin to release the judgments and interpretations that produce the anger. Guided by the Spirit, this healing can actually seem very humorous if properly perceived. The Love that the anger seemed to veil comes shining through. This movie shows how taking the lid off and allowing what is down there to arise is a helpful step towards being honest and open with communication. Although the Spirit character (Jack Nicholson) uses some pretty "unorthodox" methods for helping his student (Adam Sandler), the context is clearly for healing.

A Price Above Rubies (1998)

Whether you believe in God or not, be open to following your heart and questioning the ways of the world. Whatever you need on your journey to inner peace will appear. True religion is the experience of present inner peace, love, and freedom, not ritual and doctrine and tradition. When words and actions seem hypocritical and inconsistent, go beyond them to the experience of love in your heart.

Argo (2012) – Mind-watcher, Trusting and following

Argo is based on the "true story" of a CIA operation that "never happened." The characters trapped in Iran believe they are real people in real danger. They need help. The plan of the Spirit is to give them a whole new set of symbols set up for His Purpose, to help them escape their fearful identity and free their minds. They do not need to know how the symbols are helpful; they simply need to use them.

The crossing over from the dark dream of prison to the happy dream of freedom requires trust. The idea of escape is seen as dangerous and impossible, but when the mind is ready the Guide appears – a Guide not of this world. He knows the way; our job is to trust and to step fully into the undoing of what never was. There are times when one is called upon to simply listen and follow – without opposition – in order to save time. In this story, the window of opportunity is narrow. Delay does not matter in eternity, but it can be tragic in time. With trust, we overcome the doubt thoughts of the ego and are lifted above the battleground to safety. With each step taken, we begin more and more to perceive the common elements in all situations. The transfer of training under the Spirit's guidance increases until all guilt is undone. Trust settles every problem *now*.

A Stranger Among Us (1992)

Contrasting cultures and ethnic customs/conditioning cannot veil the bright light of true love. Love sees beyond appearances and perceived differences and draws us near. Devotion, honor, respect, and integrity are beyond the traditions of time, for these qualities touch on the Eternal. We need not conform to the limitations of time, for love is everlasting.

As Good As It Gets (1997) – Classic

There is hope for anyone and any relationship when giving way to the desire to be helpful. Opportunities to release past habits and patterns abound. When the heart finally opens, it is a glory to behold. This is a story about transforming consciousness from fear to love.

As it is in Heaven (2004) – Classic for no private thoughts, Relationships and healing

This heart-opening movie rocked Sweden and Germany when it came out in theatres. Written and directed by a master film maker who is a student of *A Course in Miracles*, this brilliant film is obviously orchestrated by the Spirit. It is the story of a famous disheartened composer who has a calling to make music that opens peoples' hearts. However, he realizes that his own heart is closed. Deep inside, he knows that he cannot run from healing. The local choir inducts him as their leader and unwittingly discover the power of exposing hidden thoughts and feelings. Turmoil seems to erupt as rigidity and conformity step aside for harmony and unity.

The ego wants things kept the same; it uses deception and the belief in sin to maintain control. But the Spirit knows that "there is no sin" and does not allow past conditioning to get in the way of opening up to a new way of living and being. Everyone in this little town undergoes changes in order to live the life they were meant to live. Abuse, fear of intimacy, jealousy, control, and competition all must be exposed so that we all can sing together with one voice.

August Rush (2007) – Classic for "The Call is everywhere if you listen," Guidance

This movie will have your heart bursting with love throughout the whole film. The Call for Love and Union is strong and the answer is inevitable. This movie is *The Song of Prayer* in action! A young boy in a boys' home has a strong calling to connect with his parents. Despite the ego's attempts to convince him he is unworthy of love and unable to hear the Call, he follows his prompts with certainty and determination. He undergoes many holy encounters as his true passion as a musical prodigy ripens within. He is to allow the music to pour through so that everyone can hear. His call is heard and answered, and the universe conspires to help him in his quest to reunite with love. No situation can be judged as good or bad, and even what seems to delay (our perceived retreats from love) is often actually essential in the ultimate plan. We must accept and follow the steps the Spirit provides to build faith so that we can see the signs that are right in front of us. Tears of gratitude are all that is left in knowing that all things work together for good.

Awakenings (1990)

The desire to help can draw one out of the shell of fears and inhibitions. In helping we are Helped. In our desire to heal and make whole, we realize we are healed and whole. Never stop hoping, for if you keep the faith the fruits of your determination will become apparent. And you will Awaken to Love!

"Charity is a way of looking at another as if he had already gone far beyond his actual accomplishments in time." T-2.V.10

Batman Begins (2005) – Vigilance, Mind Training

This movie is a classic for vigilance and mind training. Past grievances can be healed by adopting a new purpose and a sense of integrity. Bruce must learn to raise the darkness to the light in order to realize his new identity as Batman, or Son of God. He heads off to far countries to train and eventually goes home to hand over his wealth, company, and skills to a greater purpose. It takes dedication and mind training to allow the darkness to be seen truly. With service to the whole, and the desire to give over all abilities to the Spirit, we become what we truly are – certain, clear, and Self-responsible. There is no vengeance in the Spirit's purpose.

Beautiful Dreamer (2006) – The healed healer

This is a world of amnesia. A man in love goes off to war but forgets who he is when he returns to America. His wife attempts to remind him who he is but must eventually accept the way of the Spirit. The Spirit knows who you and your brother are. It simply is available and waiting for you to drop your mask and join with IT. It does not attempt to convince or change anything in the world. It is supportive and gentle and simply sees the false as false. It is patient when fear of remembering who you are is too intense. When you give up wanting your brother to awaken and simply know who he is, he joins you in the truth.

Beautiful Dreamers (1990)

Leave the ways of the world behind and dare to be unconventional. Walt Whitman guides a young doctor to a healthy mind and a new lease on life. The shift in the establishment is inevitable. Passion, openness and sharing are the ways to experience true healing. Materia medica can be left behind for the simple solution of laughter and respect.

Bedazzled (2000) – Metaphysical, Hypotheticals, Stepping stone self-concepts

Elliot, a seeming geek, believes that things would be different if only Allison loved him. He calls out "Oh God, help me please," and a sexy devil appears. Elliot is presented with an opportunity to rearrange

time, space and his self-concept in order to have a life with his unre-
quited love. No matter how extreme the hypothetical changes in form,
the experience is the same in every scenario because of Elliot's belief
in unworthiness.

With only one wish left, and having sold his soul to the devil for
a special relationship, Elliot literally finds himself imprisoned in an
impossible situation. The stepping stone self-concepts have helped to
loosen Elliot's belief in who he is. Disillusioned, he is now ready to
hear the Spirit through his jail cellmate, "You can't really sell your soul,
because it's not yours to sell." Our Innocence (worthiness) is Given;
there is nothing we can do to mess it up. It is our willingness to choose
peace instead of form of any kind that releases the miracle, returning
us to the awareness of who we are *now*. A relationship can be given to
Elliot once all desire has been handed over to the Spirit. Now instead
of being used to maintain the illusion of a false identity, it can be safely
used as an assignment for healing.

Bed of Roses (1996) – Unworthiness, Fear of love

Accepting that we are worthy of love moves us in the direction of
accepting that we are the creation of God. The denial of love is the
denial of our true Identity. This world is the denial of love. The ego
set up relationships to cover over true love and to keep the mind in a
state of fear and lack. Never receiving the love that is so deeply desired
is part of the ego's trick to keep the mind in a loop of avoiding opportunities that undo specialness and open the mind up to a love that is
not of this world. Exposing private thoughts is an essential step in the
healing of the denial. Now is the time to accept relationship assignments that are a reflection of gentleness, nurturing, and care.

Being There (1979) – Classic

True Love is innocent and beyond the judgments of the world.
Innocence is beyond fear and want, for it contains everything within
Itself. Life is nothing more than a state of mind. Mind over matter is
the lesson reflected in the final scene of this movie. In defenselessness
true safety lies; this lesson shines through clearly in the parable of this
innocent, sweet, simple gardener.

Bishop's Wife, The (1947) – Miracles, magic, and prayer

When we call out for help from God we must also believe that we will be Answered. Lack of faith is an obstacle to learning true forgiveness. Angels are all around us if we have the eyes to see. They guide us to appreciate and extend love to everyone, that we may see them all as our Self. Angels are patient and persistent, for their mission is to remind us of all the love and beauty which resides in our hearts. They help us see the valuelessness of worldly pursuits and outcomes in contrast to the value of Life in the Spirit. Their mission is complete when true love is clearly recognized.

Born on the Fourth of July (1989) – Mind-watcher for unworthiness

Anger and guilt will shift from scene to scene and place to place until its source is unveiled and forgiven within. Until there is forgiveness, the blame game, finger-pointing, and distractions to forget the pain are but follies a deceived mind plays with to stay in denial. Once anger and guilt are seen as unjustified, they can be released forever. The movie also portrays deep feelings of unworthiness.

Borrowed Hearts (1997) TV movie

Though a deceptive situation may be set up for monetary gains, God hears the prayer of the heart. Love melts the most hardened and isolated chunks of ice, and an angel hovers 'round us, often in the least suspected time and face. Any situation can be used to find the true meaning of love. The prayer of our innermost Heart, like the prayer of an innocent child, comes true.

Bourne Ultimatum (2007) – Metaphysical, Undoing false identity

Here we have yet another parable of Awakening from the amnesia of forgetfulness and false identity to the Truth of Love. On the surface of consciousness everything seems like a battle for survival in the world of bodies and seeming friends and enemies. Dark memories of the voluntary decision to separate from God have been denied and repressed, yet the world can but out-picture a decision that is kept hidden and out of awareness. The world was not only a cover-up of our True Identity, the world was also a displacement of the ego's death wish–the belief that death could triumph over Eternal Life and be acted out in form.

The seemingly guilty secret in this movie is locked away and protected in a safe in Noah's CIA office. This is symbolic of the ego's desire to hide, guard and protect the belief in death, which was nothing more than a voluntary mistake that needs to be exposed as such. The sleep of forgetfulness about the "original decision" seems to result in feverish dreams of attack and defense until the original lie has been exposed and released. Private thoughts can never be kept hidden, and once exposed it is recognized that they never had the power to enslave. Mistakes are Corrected, and the belief in death has been undone. Rejoice and be glad! Our True Identity remains unchanged.

Jason Bourne represents a fake identity, but also a mind that is in search of the truth about itself. He must first uncover and release the original lie before he can be free. Until the mind gets to the bottom of everything, it can only search. But once the lie has been exposed and released, the mind rises to True Freedom in Christ. In the movie, once the false identity of Jason Bourne has been released and the original lie has been exposed, David splashes into the water (Spirit) and is Still, and then he rises and swims to freedom. Simon Ross, Pamela Landy, and Nicky Parsons represent in the movie the desire to join in the quest for freedom and find the Truth. Noah, Ezra, and Albert represent the ego's desire to preserve itself and protect the lie. The smile on David's friend Nicky's face at the end of the movie says it all. Forgiveness prevails. Eternity radiates. True Freedom/Happiness is God's Will.

Breaking Up (1997) – Special relationship

This movie is a composite that exposes the futility of attempting "relationship" without Divine Purpose. Relationships without a Divine Aim always "break up," for they are based on nothing. Divine Purpose could be described as forgiveness–the undoing and releasing of the ego. The belief in the ego prevents awareness of True Union and Intimacy. The underlying fear of Intimacy and Union is the ego's fear of loss of itself, the "personal self" and the "personal world." There are pseudo "ego" experiences of attraction and repulsion, bonding and hatred, but underneath there is always a wish to separate and "go sepa-rate ways" or to maintain the private, independent sense of self. This is the futility and confusion of all worldly "relationships" and attempts at the "union of bodies." True Love is of the Spirit (beyond the body) and lasts forever!

Brother Sun, Sister Moon (1972) – Classic

The ways of the world and the Ways of the Spirit contrast, as darkness contrasts with Light. Love calls us inward, beneath the insane beliefs in war, commerce, and ritualistic traditions that block the Light. Love Calls, and those who hear It and follow Its beckoning find great joy that is not of this world. In following Love, the simple joys of the Spirit become apparent. Happily, in the end, darkness disappears in Light.

Bulworth (1998) – Self-concept

This movie illustrates the undoing of make-believe concepts. Like the movie *Harold and Maude*, it is used by the Spirit to undo a heap of false concepts. Included in the undoing are political, economical, sexual, and racial constructs of the self. With humor, we follow J. Bulworth as he seems to take the lid off of topics and judgments that were believed and yet unspoken. "You gotta be a Spirit, you can't be no ghost" is the reminder from the Spirit that Integrity sees beyond all judgments and concepts to the Oneness of Spirit, far beyond the ghosts of past associations and concepts. Enjoy a movie of Love and Inclusiveness that transcends race, politics, and socioeconomic status. Thanks be to God!

Butterfly Effect I and II, The (2004 and 2006) – Metaphysical for "It's impossible to change the script"

The temptation of linear time is the belief that things would be better off if they were different. The problem with attempting to redo the past is that such attempts obscure the realization that the past is over and gone. Changing one aspect of the script seems to change many other aspects, though in each attempt a whole perception that includes all situations is still lacking. Healing is seeing that all the scripts of the world are the same and therefore cannot be changed; this awareness is the forgiven world. Change your mind by accepting the changeless-ness of Mind, thus ending the loop of trying to make the world a better place or trying to save one special person. Only the mind needs salvation and it is only saved through peace. This does not require that the script be rearranged but only seen differently in the simultaneity of forgiveness.

Chances Are (1989) – Holy relationship

We are all so in love with each other, but seem to have amnesia about our Oneness in Love. In the sleep of forgetfulness we tried it "on our own," but deep inside we knew we would be back to set things straight. The roles we seem to take on in this world are where the confusion and conflict arise. These roles change and repeat in many patterns. Though every memory of the past repeats, every step on our inward journey retreats us towards our Source and True Reality. In the end, we remember how it is meant to be with God, forever You and Me after all.

Chocolat (2000) – Mind-watcher for holy relationship

The rules and rituals of "formal religion" are ego attempts to focus on the "letter" of Love while missing the experience of Love. This story is a reminder that Love does not judge, and in healing accep-tance is everyone freed from guilt. Take the stranger in. Spread the Joy of Living. Open the door to the heart and see that everyone is invited. Love blooms when it is nurtured and allowed to Be ItSelf, free from the traditions and limits of the past and far, far beyond the things of man. Be a free Spirit by extending freedom and acceptance to everyone you meet. They are your Self!

City Island (2009) – No private thoughts, Forgiveness

It is impossible to see your brother as he really is while keeping secrets and private thoughts in your mind. The family in this movie has a lot of secrets and as sometimes happens with families, they get revealed under dramatic circumstances. Do not keep your private thoughts to yourself—give them over to the light within and they will no more be seen in your world. Without exception, all the chaos perceived in the projected world is an out-picturing of an inward condition. Let's join in laughing and loving it away!

Click (2006) – Classic, Metaphysical, Exposing ego delays and bypassing steps

A man is given a universal remote control that can speed up or eliminate undesirable life situations. He attempts to use it for the ego's purposes until he realizes that the Spirit has no need to control time. Slow down and remember that any attempt to bypass or avoid certain feelings or situations is just a delay maneuver by the ego. It leads to continued distraction and eventual isolation. The momentum of pleasure seeking and pain avoidance need not be. As we accept everything that is given for the healing of the mind, time is given over to the Spirit for Its Purpose. Joy is the result.

Cloud Atlas (2012) – Mind-watcher

This movie is to be approached through meditation. Do not attempt to understand anything of this world including the past, the present, or the future. Who we are, is before time was. Many characters play out a seeming variety of experiences but all of them lead to the solution in the end. The problem was individual gain, survival, and ambition, whereas the solution is collaboration and partnership. When you give over all of your perceived needs and problems to the One who Knows, everything is given back to you to be used for awakening. Your life is not your own. End the struggle with the system by collaborating for the Whole. The characters play multiple parts. As long as you don't cling to one body or lifetime or try to even understand it, there is room to join and see beyond the separation. All that is left is love. Would you let Who You Are teach you?

Contact (1997)

Ellie Conway is a scientist who only believes in what can be proven with empirical evidence. Her deep desire for communication and exploration into outer space are her motivating interests. Without making a conscious decision to go for God, her desire for truth and her willingness to join with her companions becomes her pathway.

The ego cannot handle the Truth and does everything it can to destroy or take away the steps to the remembrance of God. God or mystical experiences are beyond the world's empirical evidence. There is nothing that can confirm the inner except the inner and it is for those who have the ears to hear. The desire to share that experience is what helps keep it in awareness until the journey's end.

As Jesus shares in ACIM, it would be unfair indeed if belief in God were necessary for awakening. Nor is belief in God a really meaningful concept, for God can be but known. Different teaching aids appeal to different people. Some forms of religion have nothing to do with God... yet if two minds join in sharing one goal, God will enter into their relationship because He has been invited to come in. In the same way joining in purpose leads to healing, being the release of separate interests.

If healing is an invitation to God to enter into His Kingdom, what difference does it make how the invitation is written? Does the paper matter, or the ink, or the pen? Or is it he who writes that gives the invitation? God comes to those who would restore His world, for they have found the way to call to Him. If any two are joined, He must be there. It does not matter what their purpose is, but they must share it wholly to succeed. Stand firm in what is Real and let not the ego tempt you to forget or shove it under the carpet. You are not Alone. It is a world of beauty as seen by the Spirit.

Copying Beethoven (2006) – Collaboration, Assignment for a higher purpose, Mystical experience

The purpose of relationship assignments is to lose awareness of separate interests and join together in a unified purpose. Collaboration is an opportunity for two minds to join as one and experience being in the Divine flow.

Beethoven receives downloads from the Spirit in the form of symphonies of music, unlike anything the world has ever heard. Ludwig Beethoven describes how the presence of God is found in the silence between the notes, and how taking down the music and playing it is as close to Creation as one can be. His direct experience of inspiration is a huge contrast to the frustration and intensity he experiences when dealing with the world. Without mind training, or a context for dealing with the ego, he is experienced by those around him as a fearful, unpredictable "force." Anna Holtz also has a calling that involves music. She recognizes the depth and purpose of a Spirit-given assignment to share in and extend the music Beethoven has received. Her willingness to be a clear, direct communication channel supports them both in going beyond their fears, into the experience of true collaboration. Pride and arrogance fall away as the Call for Love is answered.

Curious Case of Benjamin Button, The (2008) – Linear time, Undoing self-concept and bodily identification, Unworthiness

Time seems to go forward; most experience an aging process that goes from young to old as the years pass. However, awakening is undoing the belief in linear time. It is about bringing the beginning and the end together and forgiving every concept that would deny this holy instant – this moment, in which there is nothing but Love. Love is beyond the body and is untouched by age. The fear of aging and of being a burden to others is a cover over unworthiness. The Spirit can handle anything. The Spirit sees what the ego would call a disaster as nothing but an opportunity for a miracle. The script is written. The only thing that lasts is Eternal Love.

Dan in Real Life (2007) – No private thoughts, People-pleasing, Compromise

A man falls in love but soon finds out the woman he has fallen for is dating his brother. Out of people-pleasing he doesn't speak up or show what he feels, which leads to a holding pattern of private thoughts in his mind. This movie illustrates that when private thoughts are held, peace and joining is delayed. There is no need for embarrassment or secrecy. With honesty and trust, vibrational relationships can be used by the Spirit to awaken and deepen the joy.

Danny Deckchair (2003) – Opening up to inspiration

The Spirit can transform a frustrating and unfulfilling life in radical ways when the willingness and desire are there. Danny is taken away to another land by floating away on his deck chair. Even hot air balloons can be used by the Spirit to give a contrast experience that shows there is much more to life than living to work or staying in an unsupportive relationship. Through a desire to open up and serve the Spirit's function, everyone feels the blessing. It is quickly seen that the gifts of the Spirit are always what is sought and the old temptations fall away easily.

Dark City (1998) – Classic, Metaphysical

In a world of darkness controlled by time, images and roles shift and change in an ongoing nightmare, as if part of a mad experiment. Everyone seems under the spell of sleep and forgetfulness, just vaguely remembering the distant memory of light, of Home, but unable to remember how to get back there. When the plan of darkness, attack thoughts, and projection is finally uncovered and exposed, the upside-down world is turned right-side-up and bathed in the Light of Innocence in the present moment. There is no memory of a past. The games of fear and guilt are ended in the Light of True Love. Shell Beach symbolizes the Light within that everyone vaguely remembers, though the way to return has been forgotten. In the Light, Christ is recognized anew, as if for the very first time, with no memory of the past. Forgiveness is seeing that what a person seemed to do, in Reality, has not occurred.

Dead Man Walking (1995)

What faith it takes to move beyond inner fears and the seeming "opinions of the world" to find True Innocence within. What strength it takes to look past appearances and actions to the Love that resides inside, without taking sides or condemning any brother or sister. Yet faith is rewarded openly when we learn to truly forgive, and let go of the illusions that were mistakenly held about our Self and the world. We experience a joy not of this world!

Deconstructing Harry (1997)

The characters of novels and plays and movies are much like the characters that people the world. Fear and insecurity are the threads that make up the tapestry of the world. Yet as we learn not to take the people and events so seriously and have a change of heart about the world, we gain a broader perspective. We gain a glimpse of the Big Picture. Every "body" has "played the part" perfectly on the stage of the world so we could learn our one lesson. The Innocence within is all that remains when the play or movie or novel comes to an end. And when we finally learn the only lesson that needed to be learned – forgiveness – the characters offer us a standing ovation for all the gratitude and love that was always present deep inside.

Defending Your Life (1991)

The past is very much like a memory pavilion that repeats until we learn to transcend "judgment city." Fear is what holds the mind back from accepting the Spirit's purpose and having a transformation of consciousness. When the desire for joining or union becomes sufficiently singular, we are released from the past and thus released from the illusory consequences that we once believed were true. Deep down, everyone wants to love and be loved. When we relinquish fear and judgment, we at last open to the experience of True Love.

Déjà Vu (1997) Henry Jaglom

There are no accidents or chance in meetings, events or relationships. There is a Plan of Awakening, a Destiny unfolding, that ego rationality cannot comprehend. The power of Love Calls and draws us to Itself. Intuition guides us safely Home despite the many conflicting voices of the world that seem to surround us. Conventional and traditional explanations and approaches fail, but all is well. Our innermost Heart knows the Way and guides us wisely! It is a vibrational harmony of the Soul we must follow, not the "should's" and "ought to's" of convention and routine based on the past. Follow your Heart.

Devil's Advocate, The (1997) – Classic for discerning between ego and Spirit

The lures of the world glimmer and tempt toward a "better life" of more status, more money, more power, more recognition, and more sex appeal. But once these "gifts" are seen to be fool's gold, the underlying illusion of the world (ego) is unveiled. As long as one gives faith to the ego, one will seem to be a pawn in the ego's game. Once the ego exposed, it is no longer attractive. When faith is withdrawn from an illusion, the illusion disappears, just as darkness vanishes with the dawning of Light.

Eating (1990) – Special relationship, Food issues

This is a stream-of-consciousness movie in which a group of women spanning the ages of early twenties to sixties attend a birthday party. A French documentary filmmaker attends the party and becomes fascinated when none of the guests will touch the birthday cake. She begins interviewing the party-goers and they open up, revealing many hidden thoughts and beliefs, a main theme being special relationship with food. This is a great mind-watcher, or flusher of a movie. You may want to watch just a portion of it and then journal your thoughts or use an Instrument for Peace worksheet if something comes into awareness that needs to be looked at more deeply.

Eden (1996) – Special relationship, Holy relationship, Mystical experience, Sickness as a decision

Who we are is far beyond the limitations of a body. Until limiting roles and specialness are released, mystical experiences are intermittent; the contrasting experience of attempting to live in two worlds becomes literally intolerable. When the mind is no longer willing to compromise, a unified purpose becomes possible and life can become a consistent opportunity to extend love and truth. Love does not possess, nor is it proud. Love is the true healer. To love is to set free.

Ed TV (1999) – No private thoughts

Ed volunteers to be the star of a live TV show where the cameras are rolling 24 hours a day. At first the exposure is welcome and seems easy to handle, but as the cameras continue to roll, emotions begin to arise. Everyone is swept along in a rapid undoing of private thoughts, which the ego views as entertainment. The Spirit uses it all for healing, knowing that the outcome will be authentic relationships.

E.T. the Extra-Terrestrial (1982)

No matter what anyone says or does or thinks or feels or tries to achieve or accomplish in this world, deep inside they only want to go Home! It is the same lesson as the classic *Wizard of Oz* theme. Never forget this. It is the deepest desire; it is yours and mine as well! The desire to return Home is unforgettable. Call it what you will: Heaven, Oneness, Love, Bliss, Nirvana, Eternity, or Everlasting Life in God. Home is the deepest Calling of the Heart.

Elephant Man, The (1980)

Physical appearances cannot veil a kind, loving, and innocent heart. We learn that physical appearances and forms deceive until the mind is willing to look beyond them to the truth within. As with the movies *Beauty and the Beast* and *Rigoletto*, this movie offers the lesson of the inner beauty that is always present. And as the Elephant Man declares, "I am not an animal," neither is a Holy Child of God a human body. Our Reality is Spirit! We are Whole and Perfect and One, as God created Spirit in His Likeness.

Eternal Sunshine of the Spotless Mind (2004) – Classic, Metaphysical, Forgiveness of the past, Power of thought

The past repeats with private thoughts of unworthiness and doubt repeated over and over until a change of purpose in the mind is grasped. Memories of the past are deleted by the Spirit as they are offered willingly, and nothing is deleted without this willingness. Once the process is allowed with permission, only the attempt to hide some memories in the belief that they are still valuable delays the clearing. In the end, there is surrender to the Divine Eraser of past associations and meaningless private thoughts; and only the recognition of seeing the Christ anew remains Present. Staying Present, all relationships reflect the Innocence and Purity that transcends the lies of the ego. Freed from specialness, the holy relationship emerges as a testimony to the glory of God and True Love.

Evan Almighty (2007) – Classic for guidance and certainty

To remember God is to follow His guidance and instructions, even if this seems to dismantle the plans and ambitions of an imposter identity. Preoccupations with the body as well as appearances, career and image must be washed away. What better way is there than a deluge of instructions and symbols of support, to prepare for the Flood of God's Love? Without following the instructions Given, harmony, union and Love remain blocked from awareness.

Evan Baxter has just been promoted to the senate and his future ambitions to change the world tend to overlook opportunities for joining right in front of him. Following a prayer to God for help, Evan receives help that he did not expect and at first he has huge resistance to accepting the Guidance that he has clearly heard. As often happens on the spiritual journey, his family does not understand or support what he is going through, and sees the undoing of his self-concept as frightening and regressive. Eventually he moves past his embarrassment about being in communication with God and spills the beans to everyone, which results in his family leaving him.

Evan turns to his Calling with faith, following the Guidance given him, and more help turns up than he could possibly have hoped for. After some time Evan's family comes back ready to join and support him fully in the joy of being in Purpose together. The result, and continued decision to trust and join, is miraculous. With faith and obedience to what is Given, the dance party can begin. Are you ready for a miracle? Are you ready for Love?

Fairy Tale: A True Story (1997)

All the world is full of symbols for those who have the eyes to see and are open to releasing limiting beliefs. Children can be open-minded and therefore "see" what is not accessible to the close-minded. Helpers can take many forms, for form can only represent and lead to what is entirely beyond perception: Light & Love!

Family Man (2000) – Classic for undoing pride, fame, and the family concept

Jack Campbell is a wealthy, autonomous, fast-lane investment broker who believes he is living the high life. He has no idea what he is in for when the Spirit intervenes and gives him a glimpse of an alternative, relationship-focused life that requires him to develop patience, tolerance, and acceptance of what is. This film is perfect for showing the helpfulness of family for opening up to love and commitment, and putting something other than self-centered goals first. "I choose us" is the acceptance of the relationship Given now, of choosing the present and trusting that everything else will be taken care, including the future.

The ego's use of family relationships is to maintain specialness and separation, and to make an idol out of the relationships. The Spirit can use what the ego made to point towards the truth, and for deepening in communication, integrity, and intimacy. Relationships can be used to allow specialness and fear of loss to arise for the purpose of healing. As the mind opens up to the idea of sharing and extending with the whole Sonship, rather than just with a few relationships, the transfer value of what was learned in the family context is immeasurable. As communication deepens, limited family concepts fall away and the experience of love and connection can be experienced with all. The ego always resists change, because its salvation rests upon maintaining the status quo in form. Therefore the path of least resistance, one in which the Spirit's Guided changes in form are allowed and accepted, is the pain-free way to awaken. The undoing need not be painful, but it usually is so experienced.

Field of Dreams (1989) – Trust and inspiration, Holy relationship

Follow your heart on a journey of discovery. Listen to the Voice within and do what It says, even if it sometimes doesn't make sense. Your passion to discover the Truth will guide you on and draw others along with you. The whole journey is about forgiving the past and remembering the Love that is ever-present. Love waits only for welcoming and acceptance. When the heart is ready, the witnesses will appear. If you make ready the Altar of your mind, God will come into awareness. God is always present.

50 First Dates (2004) – Present moment, Holy relationship

Henry Roth is a man afraid of commitment up until he meets Lucy, who has short-term memory loss. Lucy forgets him the day after they meet, sparking a helpful journey of maturation and healing for Henry. The movie addresses the human inclination to "protect" one another from the Truth, in the name of compassion. It shows that in the end direct communication is the fast track home to God. It is symbolic of the return home to God from the belief in separation. Using mind training and mighty companions there is a way to experience freedom from concepts – Enlightenment!

Finding Forrester (2000) – Trust, Holy relationship

Seclusion and isolation close the heart away in a prison of fear. A holy relationship is born when people are brought together to learn to trust and share the Love within. The walls of fear are melted and the flame of trust ignites as the Helper within is allowed to flow through and bring help. Limitations fall to the wayside as fears and false accusations are faced head on; it becomes apparent that trust can carry one through the darkest night. Open wide and let the Love shine!

Finding Neverland (2004)

Let the dream of life be the art of playing. It is all made up so why take anything seriously. All concern for others' opinions falls away when we accept the calling to be joyful and playful. Let the Spirit take us to Neverland now, while we seem to be amongst images. The joy is always available.

Flatliners (1990)

The pursuit of knowledge for power and glory, in the name of science, is harnessed by the Spirit to bring Forgiveness to a group of cocky medical students. Delving into the mind, without being aligned in Purpose, leads to overwhelming repressed guilt and shame. Without a context of healing or a common intention, their lives begin to unravel; the projections of guilt and fear are magnified. Egoic competition becomes obviously insane; secrets and lies have devastating consequences. Yet, as the *"I know mind"* becomes more uncertain about what is real, this chink allows each one to call for help. The Spirit Answers their limited question about what lies beyond death by changing childish nightmares into visions of Innocence for all.

Forrest Gump (1994)

Innocence is unfettered by the laws and ways and thinking of the world. With faith to just take the next step, Life takes care of Life. Contentment and happiness come from non-judgment, extending love, and letting go of the idea that you really know what anything of this world is for. The journey is one of simply yielding to, or surrendering to What Is. When you give up trying to control the direction of the wind, the feather of love will gently make its way to you and land by your side.

Fountain, The (2006) – Classic for undoing time

Looking for Love in form spins out a tale of soul mates that spans centuries. The quest for the Tree of Life, which symbolizes Eternal Life, is a journey of surrender that ultimately leads to the release of the search for Love in form. While the belief that Love can be found in form persists, the desperate search produces frustration and disappointment with each seeming failed attempt. Once the fear of Eternal Love passes, the only choice that remains with regard to the book of time is to "finish it." Ascension is the awakening from the dream of form to the Bliss and Light of Eternal Life.

Frankie & Johnny (1991)

All relationship conflict arises from the personal perspective of the ego. In self-deception the self-concept/body identity is held as a substitute for True Intimacy or the Union of Mind. The belief to be questioned is the belief in fragmentation and all subsequent thoughts of rejection, betrayal, anger, and abandonment. It takes great faith to unveil what is believed to be true and to instead accept the Truth of our Self: that as a Spiritual Being we are incapable of being rejected, betrayed, or abandoned.

Frequency (2000) – Classic for communication

The willingness to communicate attracts communication, even across and beyond the barriers of time. A father and son get an unexpected opportunity to communicate across time, over the airwaves on an old broadcast radio set. Even though they are seemingly 30 years apart (1969 and 1999), they join around the World Series and collaborate on a serial murder case that spans the decades. Their strong desire to join fosters unforeseen changes in everyone's lives. Unexpected obstacles arise yet with persistence they are lead toward a happy reunion of healed relationships. The circle of Atonement undoes the challenges of time and heals perception.

Game, The (1997) – Classic for undoing the self-concept

Have you had enough of the game yet? You entered it voluntarily, although you are not sure when it began. The game seems to use everything you believe in; it reflects your desires and your fears. It plays on memories from the past. To fight against it or seek revenge will only feed the game and tighten its grip on your mind. The more you hold onto a self-image, the less likely you will be to see the game unmasked for what it truly is. Yet, though the game may seem very real for a time, in the end you will laugh at it in relief that it was never what it seemed to be. All those people were actors playing their parts. And that which believed them real was but an act as well. Game's over, Holy Child of God! Welcome Home! You can relax now.

Gandhi (1982)

Defenselessness and nonviolence are attributes of Love. Love, reflected in this world, has the power to heal all division, for separateness is the illusion. It takes determination and persistence, but for those who stay the course and transcend all obstacles, inner peace is the reward. You can see it shining in the eyes of the peaceful, sparkling in their voice, and radiating in their smile. And most of all, those that follow the path of peace become wise and wholly gentle, for they live in the Heart of God.

Ghost (1990)

An attribute of Love is communication. Like Love, communication transcends the body and remains unbroken. In its wordless state, Love is synonymous with Communion, for in Light everything is plainly revealed or Known. Love goes on and on forever; this realization comes when the lesson of forgiveness is finally learned. There is nothing else.

God is the Bigger Elvis (2012) Documentary

Deep commitment and devotion are integral to successful spiritual community, as are dedication to prayer and inner communion, backdrops for being of service, and opportunities for extension. This 35-minute documentary shows both the inspiration and the intensity of living in intentional spiritual community without worldly distractions. The nuns serving at this Benedictine Monastery are graced with Dolores Hart as their Mother Prioress. In her youth, Dolores was a Hollywood movie star who co-starred with Elvis Presley and other famous actors. When her Calling came, she turned down marriage as well as a soaring career in the movies and a million-dollar contract. When faced with the decision, she knew that there was not really a choice; "How can you explain God?"

Good Will Hunting (1997) – Unworthiness

By opening the heart and learning to trust, we learn to let go of the past and thus release the "source" of all hurt, anger, and blame. We finally open to hear the gentle voice of love remind us over and over: "It's not your fault." Only the unconscious belief, the ego, sought to place a limit on the Beautiful, Magnificent Inner Being that yearns to shine and shine. We see the Inner Beauty when we are ready.

Gospel (2005) – The story of the prodigal son

A young budding minister gets angry at his father for not giving him the attention he looked for, and runs off to a world of women and drink. When glory or growth is put first, then the truth is misunderstood. The Spirit's gifts come in stillness, patience, and and openness. Punishment is never justified.

This movie, filled with music and passion, is a modern-day rendition of the story of the prodigal son. A son who has everything, including happiness, makes a decision to leave his father's house and go about his life in his own way. He enters a world of distractions, pleasures, and conflict in order to hide from the guilt and fear that he has done something wrong by turning against his father. He returns to his father's house, where a warm welcome is waiting, but his elder brother resents his return.

The elder brother believes he has earned his father's love (even though it has really been a search for glory) and that the younger brother deserves punishment. He is envious that his younger brother gets his father's love even though he has squandered his life in debauchery. But the father teaches them both that love is eternal and unending and there is always enough to share. With openness and willingness, all can be aware of the glory of the kingdom.

Grand Canyon (1991)

The world of dreams seems fragile, hostile and unstable until we learn to let the miracle into our experience. We slowly learn to accept Help, to follow inner hunches and prompts, and to trust in Something beyond the shifting, changing scenarios. If we harbor unconscious fear, fearful dreams and fantasies seem to surround us at every turn. Yet when we let go and follow the Inner Voice of Love, symbols of joy and beauty enfold us, and we see that there have always been angels watching over us. Who can judge images and dreams as good or bad, when there is One within that is above and beyond them all. The light shines on all the world from High Above.

Greatest Story Ever Told, The (1965) – Classic

From the foretold prophecy of the messiah and savior, to the walking demonstration of Divine Love, to the extreme example of defenselessness and unbroken communion with God (Crucifixion– Resurrection–Ascension) this account is well-titled. Jesus demonstrated the potential of everyone, and much more. Jesus is a symbol of an Awakened Mind that remembers "I and the Father are One." He was called "master" by his apostles and rightfully so. For Jesus demonstrated that Spirit has dominion over the world of images and realized "My Kingdom is not of this world." He showed that is not only possible to "Be ye perfect as the Father in Heaven is perfect," it is inevitable!

Green Card (1990) – Special relationship

Out of deception and separate goals arise all tangled "special" relationships. Ego goals always produce a mask of union, for the belief in separate goals is always masked by a front. Yet the warmth of love grows and grows, and a new relationship emerges where there once was hatred and disgust. True love emerges at last in the light of truth when lies have been exposed.

Groundhog Day (1993) – Classic for undoing the belief in time

The world of time repeats over and over and over in a loop in which there seems to be no escape. Routines and activities and rituals follow predictable patterns which seem to lead in endless circles back to themselves. The desire to get something back from others leads us on a fruitless search as we seek to overcome the void inside. All attempts to escape this void seem futile. Yet when the desire to be Helpful awakens, the world is given a new purpose. Instead of focusing on escaping, we simply desire to extend and give love to everyone we meet. And with this change of purpose comes another way of looking at all the world, until we can finally say and mean "I love you." When we love from deep inside – without conditions, limitations, or expectations – the Innocence of True Love Dawns. And as this light blankets the world, we suddenly realize that we are no longer bound by time. We are free in Love!

Guitar, The (2008) – Healing

Healing involves change. What initially appears as a tragedy is often the beginning of a deep journey of transformation. Letting go of the past and accepting what is brought to your doorstep by the Spirit are powerful steps that can literally change your perception of yourself to the point where only what is truly desired remains.

Happy Feet (2006) Animated – Conformity and finding purpose

There are no rules in the world that will lead out of the world into an experience of Joy. Only answering the Spirit's call to fulfill our function and celebrate will lead to everlasting Peace. The Spirit does not attempt to conform or fit in. It just dances until everyone shares in the experience of Love's extension. Bravery to follow the calling of the heart always leads to the wonder of the Spirit. Go past the lawmakers, the gurus, and special relationships. Love will take over and supply everything that was ever needed.

Harold and Maude (1971) – Releasing self-concept

Like the movie *Something's Gotta Give*, this movie shows that age and time have nothing to do with true Love. Themes also include spontaneity, the nothingness of death, and the humor of letting go of concepts about what is "normal" and socially acceptable. A holy relationship is centered in the Present Moment, and this is what enables the transcendence of ego rituals and traditions and dogmas. Following the Spirit means playfully living in the Glory of Now.

He Said, She Said (1991)

Conflict in "personal relationship" is inevitable as long as perspectives are divided and variable. No two people see the same world or the truth inside until separate interests are laid by. When the ego enters a "relationship," competition, pride, possessiveness, and control come with it. Yet True Love prevails as light shines away darkness. And divided and variable perspectives give way to one perspective – forgiveness – in which sameness and union become apparent. What God created One remains One. Love is a unified whole and knows no differences. Love knows no opposite.

Heart and Souls (1993) – Classic

Grievance is another name for unforgiveness or unfinished business. As we learn to Help, we are Helped. This is the way we transcend the world of limits. By opening our Heart, we see that we were never bound at all. By our willingness to accept our function of Helping, we find that we have no other. Our happiness and our function are one and the same!

Holiday, The (2006) – Unworthiness, Opening up to intimacy

A workaholic and an emotional people-pleaser each need a Holy Spirit switcheroo to open them up to their hearts' desire. Whereas Amanda needs to slow down and allow herself to feel intimacy, Iris needs to release her past associations and unworthiness to allow the certainty to pour through. For Iris, this takes a willingness to say "no" and to shine her light. The Spirit uses contrasting situations to allow us to see our debilitating thought patterns and to show the joy that is possible. In the end, only love remains. In releasing relationships and situations that no longer serve, we are free to allow the Spirit to deal us a new deck, full of mighty companions that serve in awakening. The Spirit takes care of all the details.

Holy Man (1998) – Classic

In a world of advertising, sales and deception where the "almighty dollar" is worshipped, Divine Innocence can break through and shine like a bright comet in the night sky. Television seems to magnify the events and happenings surrounding a man on a mission. Focused on his mission, the holy man brings lessons of authenticity, sincerity and honesty to the forefront for everyone he meets, and assists two friends in learning to trust their hearts and open up to the Love within. With humor, grace and Presence, G demonstrates that Integrity transcends all deception and Love transcends all fear of intimacy. *Holy Man* is a modern-day parable about using everything for a Higher Purpose and laughing all the way!

Holy Smoke (1999) – Mind-watcher for fear of cults

The mystical experience of direct Union with God is an opening that will change the course of your earth experiences, sending you on a path of inward discovery toward forgiveness of illusion – Self-realization. The ego doubt-thoughts about Who You really are will seem to be reflected. You are being Called out of the world, yet initially the people who seem to surround you and the person you believe yourself to be will offer conflicting testimonies. A split mind draws forth conflicting witnesses, for it is unsure of itself and its purpose. You cannot serve two masters: Love and fear. As the goal of inner peace is firmly set, the unconscious fears and guilt will rear up in awareness. You travel inward through the darkness to the Light. In the end, it is clear to see that everything is a lesson in forgiveness. Reality is discovered through forgiveness, acceptance, and willingness to experience What Is and Forever Remains the Truth: God's Love.

Horse Whisperer, The (1998) – Classic for true empathy

Quiet inner strength comes with Integrity. Patience, gentleness, and tranquility transcend the busy distractions and fast pace of the world. With inner strength one can smile at the script, for no outcome can be fearful. And in the end there are no goodbyes, for we are One Self. The smile on the rancher's face at the end of the movie reflects the essence of true inner strength. The wise accept things as they are and do not wish they were different.

Hulk (2003)

Rage is buried deep within the unconscious mind. The rage was a false desire to make a cosmos and self unlike God, and then come up with a formula to overcome the sense of abandonment, weakness, and vulnerability. The body can never be invulnerable for it was nothing but the attempt to project error outward to form. No matter how strong and puffed up the body seems to be, the sleeping mind is simply Calling for Love. Science was made to understand that which can never be understood, and only forgiveness leads to a lasting experience of the invulnerability of Spirit. Illusions but seem to battle, yet Truth awaits only gentle recognition. Recognize the Spirit and know that Spirit and invulnerability are synonymous.

I Am David (2003) – Trust, Guidance, Overcoming guilt

Trust is the answer and this is a glorious movie of returning to our True Home. Despite what external conditions or past guilt may say about who we are, we are at home in a different state of mind that is always available. We were always innocent. Initially it can seem impossible and daunting but through perseverance, all the characters that once were threatening are seen anew as helpers along the way. The Spirit knows the way out and by following Its instruction exactly, we are led out of our prison to a new perspective and new world that was always there. At any moment we can choose to open up and see that help is available.

There are many friends along the way. Pay attention to the signs and symbols that lead to an experience of True Innocence.

I am Sam (2001) – Classic for true empathy

Who is it that is in need of healing? Lawyer, heal thyself, for thus are you Helped. Sometimes in this world the ones that seem to need the most help are the ones that allow the Help. Simple sincerity and openness and a loving heart transcend the intellectual distractions, complexity and frantic desperation of the ego. What the world calls acceptable competency in parenting skills and education is vastly overrated when these concepts are endowed with ego goals of pride, status and upward mobility. Yet, the Spirit can use these concepts when they are given over to the undoing of the ego. The simple Joy of True Love comes shining through, and the ego dissolves in the power of the willingness to let the Truth of Love be exactly as It Is. Nothing of this world can veil the Innocence of God's Love.

I ♥ Huckabees (2004) – Classic for the dismantling process, Metaphysical

I ♥ Huckabees illustrates the initial stages of awakening that everyone seems to go through – becoming disillusioned with life, looking for meaning, meeting "agents" of the Spirit and inviting them in, and, with Guidance, beginning to dismantle the perception of reality. Albert Markovsky is seeing that his way, no matter how hard he tries, is no longer working. The movie opens with the arising of Albert's doubt thoughts as he continues to try to maintain his world, aware that he really does not know if anything he is doing has any purpose. The Spirit characters (Dustin Hoffman and Lilly Tomlin) are existential detectives that help Albert change his perception of reality so that he can see the Big Picture all the time. It is only the attempt to keep some aspects of our life situation apart from the Spirit that leads to pain and confusion. It is in the relinquishment of all control to the Spirit's Guidance that we are led back home. We are all to become existentialist detectives, questioning the "nature of reality" as we know it, and welcoming the Spirit to show us another way. Everything is connected. When this is realized, there is nothing to worry about because "everything you could ever want and need, you already have and are."

Illusion (2004) – Unworthiness

Sometimes work and career can become such an obsession that they become a distraction to Loving. When hurt is buried and pushed out of awareness, life can seem like a tragedy that you just want to let end. Tapping into the Akashic records offers one man a chance to forgive his own mistakes with a son he ignored as he is given the opportunity to review his son's life and offer the Love that had been held back. If the opportunity to forgive presents itself in awareness, take it while you can. The Memory of Love remains untouched by the illusion of past mistakes. Love prevails.

Imagine: John Lennon (1988)

Imagine you are dreaming, and you forget that you are dreaming, thinking for a time that you are a rock star in a band that sweeps the land. Imagine being famous and wealthy. Imagine being adored and loathed, yet in the midst finding someone you can really share your heart with. Imagine being together, then apart, then together, then apart, all the while sharing songs from deep within your heart. Imagine that there's no problem – only a Happy Solution. So in the end you remember to watch the wheels go round and round. You really love to watch them roll. You are no longer riding on the merry-go-round. You just had to let it go. Happily you gave the world an invitation: "I hope someday you'll join us, and the world will live as One."

Imagine That (2009) – Learning to follow

"Once upon a time he was a king. But one day he left his Kingdom and got lost in 'the land of nowhere,' something no one could have ever imagined. It was a very strange place. The king was really unhappy there, he just couldn't figure out why. So those of us he left behind went out into the land to rescue him."

Evan Danielson is a financial executive who invests all of his time and energy in nowhere land, "making all his nowhere plans for nobody." Fortunately, the Spirit does not conform to insanity! The Spirit is a gentle presence calling us home, showing us how to detach from nowhere land, reminding us to invest in Love ("it's all you need!"). Evan hears the call and begins to trust what cannot be seen.

The Spirit guides us through attraction into loving relationships and opportunities to be truly helpful. He will not rip our security blanket away, but will use the images the ego made to help the mind remember that it never left the Kingdom. Symbols given over to Spirit are used as long as they are believed in. Little by little, we learn that we can make it through inner listening and in the end we see that by choosing what is truly valuable, there is no sacrifice. Here comes the Son!

Inception (2010)

The main character in this movie is looking to go home. A team is formed to help him do so. In our lives we meet people that seem to be part of our team, helping to expose the distortions in the mind – the unresolved guilt that results in the misuse of memories. We must get in touch with the guilt; it has to be healed piece by piece, through forgiveness.

A dream within a dream, within a dream, helps you forget that you are dreaming. The dream is like a maze, but there is an exit! We are the architects of the dream, and everything in the dream is a symbol. Everyone in the dream is a projection of the unconscious and will respond according to the roles we have assigned them.

Spirit, through the symbol of mighty companions, is willing to take the elevator down to the depths of the mind to help bring illusions to the light. Locked away in the basement is unconscious guilt, which persists until faced and forgiven. By forgiving the self-blame we come to realize that we have never truly harmed anyone. As we experience the increasing freedom of forgiveness we help others remember they too are dreaming.

As the players of the dark dream awaken to the happy dream they nod in silent recognition. It was just a dream; it seemed so real. We are waking up and going home! The gates that once seemed closed now effortlessly open. We finally see the face of our true Innocence and reunite with Love. And yet, even the happy dream is still a dream. Even greater Joy awaits as God takes the final step and calls us back to Oneness.

Into the Wild (2007)

Adventure and spontaneous encounters can be a path to awakening. A young man named Chris turns from society in an attempt to find the truth. In his quest he encounters many friends that help loosen him from his fixed ideas of himself and the world. The willingness to be truly helpful opens the heart and leads to joining. The search for clarity can seem to lead down many paths, and into many places, but eventually it must be seen that awakening is a completely inward endeavor and not an escape from the world. The Course tells us that all the roads of the world "but lead to disappointment, nothingness and death ... Men have died on seeing this ... and yet this was the time they could have learned their greatest lesson." T-31.IV Forgiveness of the misperceptions held about our brothers and sisters leads to the realization that we are all in this together. Joy and certainty come from inclusion in the inward journey. This is the value of mighty companions.

Invention of Lying, The (2009)

Mark Bellison lives in a world where private thoughts are expressed without hesitation or censorship. This transparency accelerates the forgiveness process, since all private thoughts, beliefs and feelings must be exposed and released. Judgments of the world maintain the belief in separation; open, direct communication sets the whole world free. In this world of private thoughts Mark Bellison tells the first "lie," believing that not telling the truth offers escape from his perceived limitations. He carries out this belief until he sees that deception never offers escape. The ego was the first "lie" or fall from Grace. All the private thoughts that seemed to follow were part of the belief in separation from God. This movie offers a glimpse into the healing power of exposing all private thoughts. Exposure leads to release (forgiveness), allowing the One Spirit beyond the private thoughts to be remembered as our True Self.

Island, The (2005) – Classic, Metaphysical

The Island is a fantastic metaphysical movie, showing the awakening process right through from being in a deceived, conforming state, to realizing that what was considered to be life was not really life at all. A society of men and women, who are deceived from birth, need to discover their true identity in this sci-fi action film. The main characters are joined in a relationship of purpose, in which they have to follow their prompts and become highly intuitive and determined to overcome the ego's attempts at stopping them from exposing the darkness. It shows the ego's temptation to go off and build a safe haven, and the Spirit's call to extend Love to everyone by going deep into the mind and flipping the "master switch" that dismantles the ego's illusion entirely, allowing the light to shine through and free everyone. As everyone opens up to the light, even those who may have seemed to be the enemy join in the celebration of innocence and freedom.

It Could Happen to You (1994) – Classic for miracles, magic, and prayer

The world is full of fairy tales and miracles! A good, honest heart. A promise that is kept. A Destiny that could not be denied. Love prevails over fear, deception and greed, for the light shines bright in a heart made ready to give. And when we give the love in our heart, the whole world is in love. Gentleness, kindness, respect, and honor follow the pure of heart. It could happen to you!

It's a Wonderful Life (1946) – Classic for miracles, magic, and prayer

The world is a funny place. When we think we gain, we forget what we have always had. When we think we've lost and that the world would be better off without us, we forget that we gave it all the meaning it had for us. Then suddenly we have a change of heart and a miracle shows us all the love we have. And when we are filled with such wonder and gratitude for everything and everyone in the world, we see the love reflected everywhere. Love prevails again and again and again. Our cup runneth over!

It's Complicated (2009) – Special love relationship, Letting go of the past

The Spirit has to find a way to gradually unwind the mind from its fixed self-concepts and limiting "comfort zones." The Spirit's purpose for relationships is letting go of the past, which is the opposite of the ego's purpose. All relationships are maximal; when they seem to end it is because they have served their purpose. Holding on to relationships and/or attempting to recreate the past maintains egoic mind patterns, rather than releasing them. Happiness and true innocence cannot be found in special love relationships. Happiness is not in the past; the past is over. It is time to let it go!

Jacket, The (2005)

We have all the time in the world to heal and transcend dreams of fear. The awareness of dreaming is the function of God's teachers and there is no time limit. The body dies, but the mind is not in the body; what the mind can do has nothing to do with the body, which can only be used as a tool.

The main character in this movie initially plays out a story of victimization. Through inner investigation, he eventually transcends the darkness and comes into an experience of being truly helpful. By learning to look calmly upon egoic fear-thoughts, Jack Starks begins to have a more unified perception of his world. He learns the helpfulness of not "freaking out" while looking at the dream of fear. This leads to clarity and deep healing of the past. Even the future is transcended when he changes his mind; what once played out will no longer be.

These song excerpts reveal the essence of this movie and Jack's final state of harmony and peace:

Quiet Inside (The Jane Doe's)
I am quiet inside
though they drag me by a wire
through the storms that cracks the sky
I am quiet inside

We Have All the Time in The World David Arnold (Featuring Iggy Pop)
We have all the time in the world
Time enough for life to unfold
All the precious things
Love has in store

Jesus of Montreal (1989)

As we commit to deepen spiritually, opportunities arise to put our faith in practice. The yearly "passion play" of the life of Jesus offers the chance to act the part for one actor, until the line between the "play" and "life" begins to disappear. Likewise, in the mystical experience there are no differences; the "act" and "actor" disappear in the Christ.

Jesus of Nazareth (1977) – Classic

O come all ye faithful to a story of transcendence of the world of dreams. "I and the Father are One; before Abraham was, I am; the kingdom of Heaven is within; I am calling you out of the world; Be ye perfect as our Father in Heaven is perfect; Blessed are the pure of heart, for they shall see God." The story of Jesus is the story of Awakening and Enlightenment. It is a story for "all times," because it is a reminder of the eternal nature of our One True Self, the Christ, which is in and of God.

Joe Versus the Volcano (1990) – Classic for trust, inspiration, and taking the leap

The Spirit awakens the sleeping mind through contrast experiences, beckoning the sleepy one to leave the past of limiting beliefs behind and trust that there is a better Way. All the world's asleep, but the Mind Awake is constantly Amazing in its vastness and grandeur! Nobody knows anything–thus the need for a miracle, a leap in faith beyond past learning and fear into the Glorious Light. The Light seems to blow the "little self" away! No matter what the apparent circumstances, One is always safely held in God's Love. All of Joe's apparent sickness came from yielding to the suggestion of vulnerability and being at the mercy of the body and world. Such erroneous thought is like a "brain-cloud," obscuring natural spontaneity and aliveness. In trusting our Intuition and following our Heart, One sees the Reflection of the Light of God and its Magnitude.

Joy Luck Club, The (1993)

False belief is projected as the world and plays out over and over in what seems to be linear time. Hurt seems to be passed on from generation to generation. Time is nothing but one past mistake replayed over and over and over. The mistake: the belief that it is possible to be a victim of something outside your self. Yet there is nothing outside the Self. This mistake is corrected in forgiveness, for forgiveness sees that mind is one and duality is illusion. The willingness to join opens the mind to the final lesson of forgiveness, which dissolves the mistake entirely.

K-PAX (2001)

A witness to a fairly advanced state of mind appears suddenly, and everyone he meets is touched in unexpected ways. Yet even this visitor witnesses to the need for forgiveness of the belief that it is possible to be unfairly treated. All Glory to God for creating Love Perfectly and as the only State of Being that there Is! Forgiveness of illusions opens the door to Eternity. How Beautiful is Spirit! How peaceful and serene and Certain.

Kate and Leopold (2001) – Trust and Inspiration

True Love must wait until the desire for autonomy fades and vanishes. In this movie, different worlds, times, and cultures seem to be blocks to connecting, yet adventures lead to an inevitable leaping off point of trust. Trust would settle every problem now. Trust that you can let go of the past and experience safety and connection and acceptance. Trust that you can seem to leave the goals and dreams of the world and share a happy dream that reflects deep Love. Trust that when you leap you will land in the Heart of Love.

Kid, The (2000) – Classic for forgiveness of the past

What you most despise about yourself must come to the surface. The perfect mirror appears and the opportunity for healing unconscious hurts is present, though not always recognized as such. Anger, frustration, and resentment can be traced to a deep seated lack of worth. This error of identity may include a false sense of superiority or pride that was built to overcompensate for and offset the believed lack of worth.

When Love beckons there is a deep Call for healing, and every scrap of guilt is exposed. Next there is a Call to join. Finally, with faith, the experience of joining breaks through in awareness and the Happiness and Love fill the Mind and satisfy the deepest longing of the Soul. The gratitude of healing flows without obstruction.

King of Hearts (1966) – "Who's the judge of what is insane?"

In a world where war is seen as reality, defenselessness and laughter and joy are often diagnosed as symptoms of insanity. Innocence has a sanity which goes beyond the accepted beliefs of the world, and in the end one must decide whether to participate in the world or step out of it. This movie "royally" exposes the farce of the world and the hypocrisy of labeling "some" as insane. Who will cast that stone, when to believe in this world at all is really worth questioning? The Kingdom of Heaven is not of this world. The Kingdom of Heaven is within.

Kite Runner (2007) – Forgiveness, Undoing the belief in guilt

See no one, then, as guilty, and you will affirm the truth of guiltlessness unto yourself. In every condemnation that you offer the Son of God lies the conviction of your own guilt. If you would have the Holy Spirit make you free of it, accept His offer of Atonement for all your brothers. For so you learn that it is true for you. Remember always that it is impossible to condemn the Son of God in part. Those whom you see as guilty become the witnesses to guilt in you, and you will see it there, for it is there until it is undone. Guilt is always in your mind, which has condemned itself. Project it not, for while you do, it cannot be undone. With everyone whom you release from guilt great is the joy in Heaven, where the witnesses to your fatherhood rejoice. T-13.IX.6

Suggested reading: ACIM Chapter 5, Section 5, *The Ego's Use of Guilt*

The undoing entails a deep journey of facing guilt from seeming past memories. The storyteller seems to experience guilt from birth, and witnesses are brought to reflect the belief in guilt and its resulting weakness. Aggression arises as attempts are made to push away guilt and shame by pushing away the brother who reminds you of your guilt. However, pushing away a brother does not remove the belief in the mind, but instead reinforces it and leads to a sense of unworthiness and loneliness. Disillusionment is experienced with the discovery that the world is based on a lie, but this brings with it a realization that this story need not be.

Through love, the guilt is able to be exposed, leading to a sense of strength and certainty and the ability to stand up for truth with those who appear to be strong and have more authority in this world. In acting from truth, a relationship unfolds through which selfless love can be experienced. The Holy Spirit is always available as a reminder that love is ever present, and finally calls us home to finish the story.

Kon-Tiki (2012)

Within all of us there is a deep yearning to answer the Call that defies all learning of the world. After World War II a Norwegian explorer embarks upon what is seen by all as a suicide mission – a journey of over 4,000 miles across the Pacific on a balsa-wood raft. Thor's belief that the ancients saw the oceans as a passageway rather than a limitation leads his inexperienced team to launch an expedition of redemption from "all the roadways of the world." T-31.IV.5 He has offered them another chance at life and each one in turn must surrender in absolute trust to the given flow of the current in order to make a safe passage. It is when our own control over the direction we are taking breaks that we can truly be steered by the Spirit.

Knowing (2009) – Undoing the world, The script is written

"And a little child shall lead them." (Isaiah 11:6) This movie shows there is a way to truth through surrendering to something greater than one's tiny self. What is perceived as insane in this world is actually a call to be Sane. Following prompts and clues lead to a way home, even if it seems backwards and upside down. This surrendering and yielding to the light happens through facing one's worst fear. This is portrayed when the female character sees that in fact her mother has been a prophet, and prophets are perceived as insane by this world. The end of the world is in the mind but it can seem as if everyone isn't ready to leave the world behind. All are called but few choose to listen.

Kumaré–The True Story of a False Prophet (2011) – Mind-watcher for spiritual self-concept

An American spiritual skeptic, Vikram Gandhi, decides to make a movie about the hypocrisy of the contemporary guru by proving to his audience that he can fabricate a guru identity and gain devotees. While many of Kumaré's teachings are purposely inauthentic, the Spirit uses everything that we made in the illusion for a higher cause. The Heart is opened through the sincerity of the student/teacher relationship; true Joining is the inevitable result of Kumaré's teachings of the mirroring principle.

Worn like a light tunic, the teacher/guru concept is laid aside and Vikram comes to the humble realization that his former followers are his true brothers and sisters. In the end, when false identity is shown to be false, the truth remains for those with ears to hear and eyes to see.

Labyrinth (1986)

After carelessly throwing away her baby brother (inheritance as Son of God), Sarah finds herself off on a quest to regain what she has lost. Mighty companions join her along the way as she goes through trials and tribulations in a world that is inconsistent and "unfair."

There is only one way to overcome the world and Sarah's real quest is to see that it is all a reflection of her mind, a playing out of her desire. Can you really be at the mercy of the ego? Is there really something or someone that can trick you and hold what you want or need out of your grasp? Watch out for her realization at the end of the movie, and the declaration that undoes the entire made-up world.

Lake House, The (2006) – Classic for undoing the idea that time is a barrier to healing

A man and a woman communicate through a letterbox while living in different years. Love has nothing to do with time. Through expression and intimacy, the Spirit collapses the past and the future. When we open up to all possibilities, the Spirit can replace meaningless relationships with meaningful ones. All present occupations and concerns dissolve in a desire to join. Time is not an obstacle to love.

Lars and the Real Girl (2007)

Fear of abandonment and fear of intimacy go hand in hand. Only a highly individualized approach to healing will allow Lars to move past his fear of abandonment and begin to open up to communication. This is a great movie for showing the mechanisms of projection, blame and holding on to grievances. The whole town rallies around to support Lars' healing process, and every step of the way it is clear that healing and release is his own decision.

Last Sin Eater, The (2007) – Classic for exposing rituals and community secrets, Mind-watcher

Forgiveness and innocence are available now. The ancient tradition involving sacrifice and rituals to absolve sins after death practiced by her fellow villagers is unacceptable to a young girl, burdened by the weight of her "sin." Her plight for forgiveness sparks off a chain of events that lead to the exposing of the deep, dark secrets that have been protected and harboured by the villagers for many years. The decision to face the darkness and expose the belief in sin leads to the miracle of healing.

L.A. Story (1991)

Laugh at the idiosyncrasies and extremes of this world as the main character learns to trust and follow Guidance from an unusual channel (a freeway message board). A love story about following Guidance and letting destiny take its course. In the end the power of love prevails and reflects the strength and magnitude of our One Source. Never give up on Love!

Last Station, The (2009)

Even Tolstoy is not a good Tolstoyan. When Tolstoy gets a new secretary the compromise between his beliefs and his actual life come into sharp focus. Many thousands have begun to follow the man but in doing so, has the principle of love and freedom been lost? This is a film about experiencing the movement in the mind from one of following an ideal towards one of living a life of Freedom and Love. Asked to be Tolstoy's new secretary, Valentin is put in an observer role; he keeps parallel journals reflecting the public and private personas of one devoted to experiencing the Truth. Through the intimacy of this assignment he is given a unique opportunity to discover what is truly important. Aided by Masha, who symbolizes the spirit of the movement, Valentin explores following the letter of the law versus the spirit of the law.

Tolstoy's wife is simultaneously Tolstoy's biggest support and his greatest downfall. The special love, faith and devotion that had once been used by the Spirit to support the dissemination of the message is now being controlled by controversy and compromise. But Tolstoy's belief in loyalty to his wife *and* devotion to his cause has him split and weakened. Persons do not become enlightened. Follow the "way," not the man.

Leaving Normal (1992) – Trust

A journey of trust and letting go of the past. Taking off on a trip and letting it unfold, learning and growing from "relationships" and encounters along the road. Our two main characters are so open to Guidance that they hold open a map and go where the bird droppings land on it! A movie about forgiveness and letting go of inner pain and expectations.

Legend of Bagger Vance, The (2000) – Classic for guidance

This is a story of faith and trust and of being willing to receive and accept Guidance and Love. Randolph Junuh is disillusioned with life and has deep feelings of unworthiness. The Spirit reaches him using a backdrop that is familiar and attractive to him. The metaphor of "you have lost your swing" is the metaphor for "you have forgotten who you are." The Spirit uses golf as a backdrop for discovering his authentic swing, which involves getting out of the way and allowing it to find him.

The way back to remembering Truly is through joining, deepening in trust, and listening to Guidance while using learned skills and abilities. It is then possible to go beyond all of what is learned to an experience of harmony with all that is. The path of healing is one of coming into integrity. Facing "demons" from the past allows one to step up and play.

The opportunity is always one of forgiving all doubts, fears and limitations and allowing the Real You to Shine through. Once the world is glimpsed as meaningless, the lesson of inner discovery has begun. Yet the aim of forgiveness is to see the false as false so that the True Meaning of Spirit can be accepted exactly As It Is. The angel appears in form as an Answer to the prayer of the heart. The angel is steadfast in the Purpose of release. And the angel will seem to stay until the lesson can be accepted and applied. All Glory to God for all the Divine Help in Awakening!

Letters to God (2010) – Miracles, magic, and prayer

This is a movie about hope, prayer, and purpose. Has the word prayer ever been used this much in a movie?! A young boy with a terminal illness starts writing to letters to God as a form of prayer. He encourages everyone around him to do the same, and in doing so, minds are turned towards God as a Source of comfort and communication. The boy's letters are given to the local postman, who is going through his own life struggles. After asking the local pastor what to do with the letters, he is told that they are part of his own journey with God. The healing is for all, and the desire for healing and connection with God radiates out, inspiring the whole community.

Let It Ride (1989) – Classic

A story of faith, trust and destiny. Intuition guides and with willingness to follow, our experiences lead to a further opening of Inner

Guidance. Decisions flow from which inner voice we listen to (ego or Spirit) and our state of mind reflects the mind's allegiance to illusions or truth. Regardless of the world's appearances, when we follow the Spirit we are happy.

Life as a House (2001) – Classic for rebellion and parenthood

A typical American family has suppressed rage and past grievances that cover over compassion and love. It takes what the world calls a serious situation to see that there is much more to life than struggle and depression. This is a fantastic story of transformation and redemption through humility and communication. The whole family goes through an experience of forgiveness and healing as they join together to work on a long-awaited house-building project. Deep feelings of rage and abandonment are exposed, leading to feelings of hope, joy, and love. Love is content, not form.

Lilies of the Field (1963) – Purpose, Accepting one's function

In the midst of ultra-small-town America, there is every opportunity for the Holy Spirit's plan to unfold. Bypassing all cultural and language differences, this movie aims at the undoing of control and submitting to a Higher Plan. Even though there are many attempts to come to agreements and stick to bargains, it is only in following the Spirit's plan that a sense of Purpose and Joy is felt. Following the Plan will allow for all worldly agreements to be used with integrity. There is no purpose in reciprocity, and the Spirit will use all that you seem to have in this world to undo it. It wants to have the mind learn that, "To have, give all to all." T-6.V.4 The character Homer Smith undergoes a transformation of working for who and when he wants, to seeing that all things are done by the Holy Spirit and for the Holy Spirit. With the church as a backdrop, he gets to see the ego's desire for credit and its unwillingness to accept help. He projects his own control onto the head nun, but in the end, her certainty and faith bring him into alignment with what serves the whole. When a task is given, the mind's only responsibility is to follow the instructions. The Spirit will provide the means. All that is left is an "amen" to the Holy Spirit's gentle plan of surrender.

Limitless (2011)

For the mind asleep and dreaming, waking up seems to demand a loss. Eddie Mora has spiraled to an all-time low; an ex-addict and blocked writer, he is mocked by what was once great potential. Recently jilted by his beautiful and patient girlfriend, he has failed according to the world. When offered a new designer drug as a gift, he has nothing to lose – except all the doubt thoughts that have held him back his entire life! This new mind-expanding portal lifts Eddie into unprecedented clarity. "I knew what to do and exactly how to do it."

The little willingness to step out of smallness is all the Spirit needs. The belief in the power of drugs is used to open the mind to unlimited opportunities for forgiveness. After a period of grandiosity it is obvious that "an untrained mind can accomplish nothing." W-in.1.3 Discipline is required to maintain razor's edge perception. Resistance to magnitude is reflected as Eddie begins to meet others who have withdrawn into littleness and fear after the initial high of taking the drug. They seem to manifest a mysterious illness as they retreat back to the perceived safety of limitation. But, once Eddie turns his newly found attentiveness towards a greater purpose, Spirit can guide him towards true helpfulness and service. Once the mind is freed from belief in attack, lack and reciprocity, the experience of limitlessness transcends the need for the drug; it was just a stepping stone. This is a glorious movie for getting a taste for the release from belief in limitation.

Lion King, The (1994) Animated – Classic, Metaphysical

A parable about being given a kingdom, then being tempted to look outside your kingdom, then believing a lie that you killed your father, then taking on the guilt and blame of the lie, then running away from your kingdom out of shame and trying to forget a past believed to be real. Finally you are called on to return and face and overcome the guilt of the past and remember your rightful inheritance in the present. The kingdom of our perception is bleak and dark if we hold onto guilt and shame. When we forgive our self and realize what we thought we did never happened, we remember the glory of the Kingdom of Heaven.

Lion King II, The (1998) Animated – Classic

Seeking again outside the kingdom results in the perception of war. The war ends when we remember that we are all the Same One, laying aside the belief that we are separate and different. Love brings an end to all conflict, for what is One looks on Itself with Love and sees no differences.

Little Buddha (1993) – Mind-watcher

The story of Siddhartha's journey to Enlightenment symbolizes the desire to transcend the cycles and trappings and temptations of the world. Birth and death, attraction and repulsion, success and failure seem to repeat over and over and over until they are seen as illusions. The Awakening occurs when the mind sees past the illusion of the body/world "self" and recognizes One Self as Spirit. The search ends in finding and experiencing One Self. Oneness transcends duality.

Little Princess (A Little Princess, 1995 / The Little Princess, 1939)

A little girl adored and loved by a father who sees all little girls as princesses appears to be separated from him. She undergoes harsh experiences during the time she seems to be without her father, but keeps her faith that she and all little girls are indeed princesses. In the end her faith and desire to join with other little girls is rewarded as she overcomes all doubts and hardships and is reunited with the father she thought she had lost forever. A parable paralleling the seeming "fall from Grace" and the inevitable Awakening to our True Identity in God.

Looper (2012)

Joe, a killer who works for the mob, is stuck in the loop of time. To avoid his impending death, he tries to bend the rules of his personal world. But in order to truly escape death (and the desire for murder), he has to see that death *is* the idea of time. When the lost, unwanted child is still present in the mind, no amount of money or worldly success can hide or eliminate the pain. Unworthiness and self-hatred need to arise in order to be released. Relationships provide opportunities to see things differently, and only by leaving the battleground can you see that love is what finally ends the loop of time.

Lord of the Rings: Fellowship of the Ring (2001) – Mind-watcher,
Collaboration

This cinematic masterpiece is a story about joining together in a common purpose. It does not matter what your capabilities are in this world, the Spirit can use them all. It may seem that we head off on separate paths, but in the end we join together to recognize that the Brotherhood, or Christ mind, could never lose. The ring of form is cast back to where it was forged and freedom is remembered. We all played our parts perfectly. Only when we give up separate interests and ignore the temptation of false power can we accomplish our goal. It may seem to take the path of a long journey, but all things work together for good. Gollum is seen to play his part perfectly when judgment is removed. Gandalf demonstrates there is no death. Aragorn reminds us that our true inheritance can be remembered and that we are worthy. Legolus demonstrates loyalty and singleness of purpose. The hobbits remind us we are never to take anything seriously. There is always a miracle waiting for us when we accept our function.

Love Actually (2003) – Classic for opening up to intimacy and no private
thoughts

This is a powerful movie that has every scene maximized for healing. All thoughts are expressed and hidden secrets exposed, which leads to healing for all concerned. People-pleasing and fear of intimacy go hand in hand. When we choose one, we get the other. A scared office worker, in love with her co-worker, fails to open up her heart due to the fear of leaving the perceived "safety" of her family obligations. Many different stories collide in this romantic comedic drama. The airport scene at the end pulls us back to see all these stories as the past and "on the screen." The happy dreamer gives no special importance to any specific relationship, but allows the Spirit to use them all maximally. It is not concerned with status or rank as the world judges. Every relationship can be used by the Spirit as they all give us the possibility to remember who we are.

Love Affair (1994)

A man vows to change his lifestyle and meet the woman he loves at a prearranged date on top of the Empire State Building. She agrees to meet him. They promise that if either doesn't show up they will get on with their lives without contacting one another. On the prearranged date, he shows up but she is hit by a car while en route to the building and seems to lose the use of her legs. She is too ashamed to let him know what happened, and does not contact him. But love and destiny bring them together as love and destiny bring us all together in God. When what we are ashamed of is revealed and brought to Light, the love in our hearts shines forth unencumbered. We are worthy of being loved regardless of the appearances of the world. Have faith and never hide your deepest feelings of Love!

Made In Heaven (1987)

Those who are destined to meet will meet. As we follow our heart's desire, God's Divine Plan unfolds. As we desire to help, we are Helped. If we keep the faith through all the doubts, our faith is rewarded. For All of Heaven is offered us now. And when we are willing to open our hearts and minds to the light of Love, we will experience the deepest prayer of our heart: A love that lasts forever!

Man Facing Southeast (1986)

A psychiatrist is brought face to face with his despairs, fears and perceived limitations through an encounter with a "patient" that is not of this world. Rantes, the patient/teacher/learner, is on an earth mission of compassion, and the "fellow patients" around him are drawn to his calm, healing presence. In the end the psychiatrist must decide, as each of us must decide, what/who is insane and what/who is sane. If the entire ego world is a hologram of insanity, only a mind given to (Spirit) forgiveness can find peace. Projection makes perception, and the mind perceives what it believes. The only way to let go of insanity is to stop believing in it by rising in consciousness to meet Truth. Love and Truth are One Spirit.

Man Who Knew Too Little, The (1997) – Classic

Once the suggestion "all the world is a stage" comes to mind, the path of true forgiveness dawns. Forgiveness is nothing more than seeing the false as false and therefore not taking any of the persons, events, and situations seriously. How light and humorous is a world of actors at play in a play. How defenseless and fearless is such a Perspective of the world. Nothing is taken personally when all situations are viewed as play-acting. There is nothing to fear when the world is seen as merely a theater of actors, actions, and events.

In *The Game* the main character symbolizes being unaware that everything is all a game of actors and seems to buy "the bait." In *The Truman Show* the main character symbolizes becoming suspicious of the world which seems to surround him and then, with great determination, arrives at Point of Decision and realizes It is the Point of Escape. In *The Man Who Knew Too Little* the main character is an example of an ongoing experience of this (beyond all fear) Perspective, which is continuously available and accessible. The script is already written. The joy is in the Perspective you view it from.

Mask of Zorro, The (1998)

I want to spend my lifetime Loving You. A theme of this movie is the question of the world: Who is my Father? The ego offers many answers to this question, because the ego is the belief that it is possible to author or create one's self. Forgiveness shows that this is impossible, and the doubt about source/origin is ultimately put to rest as the Source is discovered to be God. This is a love story about going past mistaken identity and pride, exposing error, and accepting that you are worthy of Love. The theme song at the end is inspired: Seize the day, stand up for the Light. I will want nothing else to see me through, if I can spend my lifetime Loving You.

Matrix, The (1999) – Classic

You are the One! Free your mind from a world of control based on limitations and fear. The matrix is everywhere, for the matrix encompasses all appearances and images you seem to perceive. What if you were unaware that you were dreaming? What if you could not tell the difference between the dream and the real world?

The matrix is your seeming digital "self," a projected image of a mental construct called ego. The matrix is a construct that can seem loaded with all sorts of erroneous ideas of attack and defense. One choice (ego defensiveness) leads to continued imprisonment for your mind and you seem to remain asleep and dreaming of the matrix. One choice (Spirit) shows you how deep the rabbit hole goes and frees your mind to forgive illusion and recognize Its Oneness, thus accepting your own Saviorship. Follow the White Rabbit (the Spirit). No one can tell you what the matrix is, you have to find out for yourself and be lead inward to the experience of your True Christ Self. I can show you the door (forgiveness), but you have to walk through it. You are the Savior of the world as you let your mind be free of the ego belief system and its limits. There is nothing to fear. Your Destiny is Certain. You are the One. No one can fail who seeks to reach the Truth.

Matrix: Reloaded, The (2003)

(Anomaly: the state or fact of being out of place, out of true, or out of a normal or expected position; deviation from the normal rule.) Love is the only Law or Rule, since God is the only Source and God is Love. Release from illusions is not found in war, but in forgiveness. As long as there seems to be an "enemy," the Self remains unrecognized. The architect of specialness, the matrix is the ego, and all seeming options and decisions and outcomes in form are part of the matrix. Every decision is already made and there is no choice among illusions. As long as you believe that there is some "body" to fall in "love" with or to "rescue," the matrix will seem to continue in sequel after sequel. When there seems to be a construct to protect or save or defend, the belief in separation is still held dear. Yet release is always available and, in fact, has already been accomplished. You need but accept what is already Present. Welcome Home!

Matrix: Revolutions, The (2003)

Battle gives way to acceptance and joining, a surprising simple Solution to the impossible situation called the matrix. Atonement is the simple Solution. The ego was the illusion of complexity. The Solution cannot be found with the "physical eyes," yet the Inner Guidance of the Spirit directs the way to the Certain Solution. The overcoming of error is simply the awareness of its unreality. Love is Real and Love has no "opposite."

In the end the "architect's" game of error is laid aside and abandoned, because it was never real to begin with. And the happy, bright world which forgiveness shows is bathed in Innocence. The oracle of Truth and the child of Innocence rest side by side as a symbol of the forgiven world. Peace and Light have spread across the matrix, and Now only the Light of Love is reflected throughout the whole tapestry. It is true: You are the One. Know Thy Self. No one can tell you Who You are, You have to Know It for Your Self! The matrix could never tell you Who You are, but the Voice for God is gently, ever Lovingly reminding. You are the Living Christ, Beloved of God. You are forever the One!

Meet Dave (2008)

This funny movie brings to light the eccentricities and nuances of human life. Dave comes from outer space. He is a spaceship in the form of the Eddie Murphy character. He has his crew with him and they collaborate in a way that can be seen as holy relationship in action. Filled with metaphysical nuggets this movie demonstrates that following your heart can be fun and expressive!

The voice for God is always in the mind, extending a hand of collaboration and good will. The other voice, the voice of plans, pillaging and personal gain is also always in the mind until one voluntarily decides to decommission it. The body is a communication device and responds as the mind directs. Things get disastrous when the steering wheel is given over to the ego. Keeping the joining out in front will allow the Spirit's solution for all to shine through.

Meet The Fockers (2004) – Mind-watcher for no private thoughts

Meet the Fockers is the ultimate people-pleasing movie. Gaylord Focker attempts to join with and impress his future in-laws when meeting them for the first time. His people-pleasing antics are a recipe for self-doubt and uncertainty. Every dishonest response and attempt to be liked backfires until finally there is no option but to come clean and bring an end to the approval-seeking fiasco. The only thing that makes any sense is love and with the willingness to be direct. When this is the case, the witnesses turn from suspicious to supportive.

Meet the Parents (2000) – Mind-watcher for people pleasing and no private thoughts

In *Meet the Parents*, it is time for Gaylord's fiancé and her family to meet Gaylord's parents. Although the people-pleasing has lessened a little, Gaylord continues to compromise in an attempt to make his parents appear normal and acceptable to his judgmental future father-in-law. There are lessons in trust for both Gaylord and his father-in-law. Their attempts to keep private thoughts wreak havoc throughout the weekend until they both realize the importance of honesty and extending what they wish to receive.

Mind the Gap (2004)

In this beautiful movie ancient grievances are transformed into healing encounters through joining and communication, demonstrating the importance of being open to Forgiveness and seeing that the past need not hold any power over us *now*. Several characters have deep emotional wounds that are covered over and run their lives. One almost commits suicide, while another wants her tubes tied because of past associations. Two are frightened to be in a relationship, and another is scared to go into the city. Through synchronicities and a willingness to open up and be vulnerable, their True Invulnerability is seen. Then the next steps that lead the mind deeper into joy are given obviously and easily. True Forgiveness is highlighted in a scene where a father asks for forgiveness from his young son and the boy just says, "Ok, Daddy," with complete detachment from the idea that there ever was a past to forgive.

Minority Report (2002)

The topics of telepathy, time, events and choice are rich with insights. Time and events were a prearranged script that is already over and done and must be seen as such (forgiven) for healing and peace of mind. The ego's perspective is a lens of crime, abuse, deception and murder, and this lens or perspective is the error of death. This lens sees time as real and unfolding, with events as real, and the past as different from the future. Forgiveness exposes the entire time line as the lie, and offers the mind the choice of Atonement (seeing that the separation never happened). Atonement is the gateway to the remembrance of Divine Innocence as a Perfect Child of God in Spirit. Forgiveness is the option that transcends the insane desire for revenge that was based on the belief that mistreatment and death were real. Forgiveness sets the mind free, for the mind has thus escaped the belief that it must run and hide or prove its Innocence.

Mirror Has Two Faces, The (1996)

The fear of Intimacy is exposed in this "exploring the meaning of relationship" comedy. The anxiety and fear related to body identification, expectations, desires, body-image, coupleness, and body-ideals is presented in depth. The attempted "platonic" relationship is an experiment which, though cautiously approached, seems to spin from attraction to avoidance. Any and every relationship believed to be "personal" will eventually be undone. The only Real Relationship is Being One with God. Until the mind releases the body identification, relationship seems to be between persons and True Union (the One Mind) is feared. True Love is abstract, impersonal, and unconditional and is revealed after all that Love is not has been exposed and released. True Love is beyond the body.

Mr. Deeds (2002)

Deception in a relationship always gets exposed, sooner or later. The lures of money and power and fame make deception seem like a small thing, but tiny "white lies" can seem to add up. Yet deception melts in the Presence of simple honesty, and Love remains Loving. In the end only Love is real and Simplicity transcends all complexities and conflicts. Ask that Life Be Simple and experience the Simple Answer. Give simple honesty another chance, and watch the miracles unfold.

Mr. Destiny (1990) – Classic for giving up control, Metaphysical, Serenity Prayer theme

The central problem of the world could be characterized as the belief that things would be better if circumstances in life or events of the past were different. The main character in this movie believes his life would have turned out better if he had just hit a home run instead of striking out in the last at bat of his high school baseball team's state championship game. A spiritual guide in the form of a bartender appears to help him see the truth beyond his wishful thinking.

We shall come to learn to be grateful for everything in life and to trust that indeed all things work together for good and that all events, situations, and circumstances have a Purpose behind them. We can choose to be happy and grateful regardless of circumstances, for our state of mind is always a decision. As the guide says, "I make the suggestions; you make the decisions."

My Best Friend's Wedding (1997)

We never "win" love through deception. The main character tries vainly to "win over" the love of her best friend before he marries another woman. Yet in the end all lies are revealed and seen as futile gestures, for True Love is beyond all deception. And a true friend will tell you the truth, even when you don't want to hear it, and always be open to help in times of need. The Spirit within is always our True Friend.

My Dinner with Andre (1981)

A simple dinner conversation can be a profound encounter and lead to feelings of connectedness and joy! When there is a desire to go deeper than the mundane and ordinary, a desire to go beneath the surface chatter and banter and delve into the real, a vibrant experience is available. This movie demonstrates how a dinner conversation can inspire, and reminds us that there is more to life than the commonly held assumptions and opinions. A mind that will question the assumptions on which the world is based is on its way to discovering the Real. Reality is beyond belief, beyond opinions, and beyond judgment. Discovering Reality can be an adventure!

Next (2007) – Classic for undoing time, accepting one's function, and following guidance, Metaphysical

What if everything that seemed to play out was just hypothetical? What if every potential possibility could be seen and the mind could zoom in and select which scenario to play out? Chris Johnson has a physic ability that allows him to do this and yet, without any real sense of purpose, his life is one of hiding and pretense. The Spirit uses attraction and a guided relationship to get his attention and open him up to seeing that through joining he can go beyond his fears and expand his perception and abilities. This great movie reminds us that no matter how many ways we look at trying to change the future, we must find out that only a change of Purpose is the answer. The whole world is hypothetical, and when this is seen there is surrender. The script is written, and there is no point in trying to figure it all out. Just rest and join with your brother to end the past. It is all forgiven, and at any point you can choose again for the Plan of the Spirit.

Nines, The (2007)

A symbol for a potential far greater than what we currently experience, the Nines are those that have unlimited power and can create worlds with a single thought. The main character really believes that he is a man and inside a "real" world. He has forgotten that this is all a computer simulation; he is playing characters that he himself designed. Through multiple lives he comes to learn to see the patterns that are holding him back. Specialness is the key defense; Spirit must "get him away from her." She is like a drug, as are his family and friends. In order to cover up his "drug of choice" he hides himself in addictions, a rebel attitude, and his work. Finally he learns the difference between what is true and what is false. His world(s) begin to unravel and the Truth is revealed. Enjoy this movie, especially the final decision!

No Reservations (2007) – Classic for letting go of control

Control is impossible. The illusion of it blocks the awareness of love. A young, stubborn head chef is caught up in her work as a defense against the present moment. The Spirit must work miracles by restructuring her environment and sending her a child and sous chef to open her heart. What the ego views as disaster, the Spirit interprets as an opportunity to open to an experience of joy. Competition perpetuates fear and leads to isolation, but a willingness to see that we are all joined in this together opens the mind to heart-warming collaborative ventures.

Oblivion (2013)

This futuristic movie centers on Jack, a veteran assigned to extract Earth's remaining resources for a surviving human colony that has been relocated to another place in the cosmos. Jack and his partner Victoria try to stay focused on their mission at hand so that they can join the colony, but memories from Jack's past begin coming into his awareness. As unexpected and startling events unfold, Jack begins to question everything he knows about his mission, himself, and his partner. Nothing he has believed is true, and the memory of deep Love is remembered after Jack discovers that a woman he rescues is in fact his wife. The memory erasure covering the deception of control and a false world is exposed once and for all, and Jack plays his part in breaking free of the lie. True Love cannot long be denied; false memories always give way to the Truth of Love.

Only You (1994) – Classic for "you can't mess it up!"

We are always in the right place at the right time, and this is so, no matter how twisted and convoluted the journey seems to be or how we travel. Our Heart Calls to us and we receive signs that lead us onward toward our final Destiny in Love. We move closer when we do not settle for "should's" and "ought to's" and remain open to the signs along the way. Deception threatens to throw us off course, but if we remain open, we find that what we had been searching for was right here all along. It was only our doubts that temporarily led us astray. Whatever will be, will be. Those who are destined to meet will meet. And in the End we shall all meet in the Divine Experience of Love.

Original Sin (2001)

What is sin but the error of deception, and what is Salvation but acceptance of the Correction to error? Sin seems to be acted out in form, in flesh, yet the error is simply an erroneous belief which seems to yield a faulty formulation of reality. Sin is a mistake to be Corrected, not a black mark that can never be erased. The "original sin" was the belief that separation from God was possible. It seemed to be enacted in deceptions of the flesh, yet there is a Perspective of non-judgment Which overlooks the error entirely and sees only Truth. Forgiveness releases the mind from the repetition of the original error, and in this release is true freedom, peace, love, and happiness. Only Original Innocence remains Now.

Other Boleyn Girl, The (2008) – Mind-watcher for jealousy

Ambition leads to folly and pain. At any moment the decision can be made to rest from worldly goals and experience the simplicity of the present moment. All attempts to increase status, wealth, or security lead to demise whereas the Spirit simply flows in the moment. Symbolically, in this movie, the rest and joy of a simple life in the country is given up for the possibility of power in the city. Jealousy spawns deception and ends in death. This is an extreme example of "childhood trauma" and shows that all of the ego's stories are the same no matter what time or location they seem to take place in. Spirit's plan is here now when we recognize the script of the world cannot be changed. Why not rest, relax, and enjoy, and see that our Kingdom is not of this world.

Passengers (2008) – Life is a dream that you made up

Everything we seem to experience is only an act taking place in our own mind. Fear makes you dream a dream of being a person with certain characteristics. You may be using an occupation for the making of an identity and even this the Spirit will use for the healing of the mind. There are many helpers along the way. You need to have the courage to face the fearful thoughts of the past and welcome them into awareness. This allows you to heal and to see that you were only dreaming and that everyone was there to help you. You just perceived them wrongly.

Passion of Mind (2000) – The power of thought

Alternate dreams can seem to offer something of value to the dreamer when desire is split or multiple. The nagging sense of separation beckons the question: "Which of these dreams is reality?" Yet Reality is only approached when conflicting dreams are brought together and forgiveness shows that all the dream figures were aspects of mind. The roles in conflicting dreams were but shadows that veiled the True Self, and in the dream everyone and everything is symbolic. Peace comes at last when it is apparent that there is nothing outside the mind.

Paycheck (2003)

This world is about getting something for nothing. We always look to maximize the gain with a minimal payout. The Spirit's way is different. It is about giving all to all. In order to reverse this direction, one must be convinced that there is another way. Michael Jennings is going after the big paycheck that will secure his future by giving up time now. His plan fails. He sees that the more he invests in the future the more the future is like the past, full of greed, corruption and death. A holy relationship is given him to see the valuelessness of this frivolity. While seemingly committed to undertaking what he has started (an unholy alliance with time and concern for the future), he learns that there is a way out – a way that he himself set up before time began. In an attempt to break free from the cycle of reciprocity he must follow the clues and use the means given to him by the Spirit (his True Self). He sees that the script is written and that he cannot get it wrong. As he flows along there is a temptation to see into the future again but this is just a distraction. He must go to the source and shut it down so that he can be present. The ego has no chance in a mind that has no self-interest. He is freed from the cycle of death; all that he thought was lost was returned to him without the burden of trying to *get*.

Pay It Forward (2000) – Classic for giving and receiving are the same

Experience that true giving and receiving are the same. What you have been given by a teacher or a brother you can keep by giving it away to others. That is actually the only way that you can keep it. Teach what you would learn – teach true generosity by always extending love.

Phenomenon (1996)

Our capacity for learning is enormous. If we are eager and open, learning can take us higher and higher in consciousness. We may seem to develop abilities of mind that are natural, but that can seem super-natural to the world and people around us. Do not be afraid of true intimacy or of that which you cannot explain scientifically. For as you rise in awareness of Who You Truly Are, you will develop abilities to such an extent that they will release you from an impossible situation. And this world of conflict and guilt and fear is an impossible situation. You will Awaken to the Eternal Reality of your Self in God.

Phone Booth (2002) – Intense mind-watcher, Undoing self-concept, Exposing deception and private thoughts

The self-concept is made up of lies. It manipulates constantly to maintain its (shaky) self-image. It is a cover over the deep fear that what is underneath is unlovable. The call for self-honesty is also very deep, and the exposing of the lie can seem extreme and traumatic. It is like facing the threat of death, and it isn't over until all of the darkness is raised to the light for release. "Coming clean" makes space for who we truly are to begin to emerge. Rather than being rejected for exposing the ego, love rushes in immediately, and the opportunity for a real relationship finally becomes possible.

Peaceful Warrior (2006) – Classic for teacher/student relationship

This is a brilliant movie about a young man who meets an unlikely spiritual guide and goes through a rapid awakening that involves facing and releasing the ego while turning to the inner strength and focus that is found in the present moment. What the world calls brave and strong is actually a facade over fear. The Spirit works with the mind to develop true strength. Through trust and discipline, the teacher and student can collapse time to awaken to the truth of our equality. It is a masterpiece in showing where true healing lies and that all sickness is judgment and faulty perception. Enjoy the simplicity and strength of living with one purpose.

Pinocchio (1940) Animated – Classic for autonomy

The story of the quest to be real. The goal requires the development of honesty and integrity—learning to be truthful. The distraction of "pleasure island," an alluring temptation where things are not what they seem, is the obstacle to be transcended. This movie is a lesson in discernment, learning which voice to listen to and trust.

Pocahontas (1995) Animated – Classic for guidance

Listen to your heart and you will understand. It takes determination to listen to your heart in the midst of expectations and voices from the past. Love transcends cultures and traditions, which must always clash. The desire for peace and harmony brings resolution to conflict. If open to inner guidance, the direction is pointed out to a mind willing to listen.

Pocahontas II (1998) Animated

For a time it seems as if putting on appearances is a way of gaining something. But in the end the realization dawns that we can only be Who We Are and have nothing to be ashamed of. True Love transcends cultures, roles, status, and skin color, for love is everlasting. Contrasts in cultures and values dissolve when true value and meaning is finally grasped.

Pollyanna (1960) – Miracles, magic, and prayer

Pollyanna is a budding miracle-worker. She is in her function, joining with everyone she meets. Although her "positive attitude" isn't always welcome, her optimistic approach is a deliberate attempt to see things differently. Abraham Lincoln said, "When you look for the bad in mankind expecting to find it, you surely will." Hence Pollyanna's commitment to look for the good.

Powder (1995) – The power of thought

The world is afraid of what it cannot understand, label, and categorize. Powers and abilities of the mind that go beyond accepted norms, as well as appearances that stand out, are both judged harshly. Yet the development of powers, abilities, and appearances that defy traditional explanations are natural phenomenon as the mind evolves beyond limiting beliefs. The greatest desire of our hearts is to go Home, to go back to the Source of our Being.

Preacher's Wife, The (1996)

A modern-day version of *The Bishop's Wife*. When the specifics and organizational concerns of the world become our "church," a drift away from our True Focus seems to occur. This is called by some "losing faith." But with some Divine Help answering the prayer of the heart, we are guided back to what is truly important. When the True Focus is our number one priority, all things are seen aright.

Premonition (2007) – Mind-watcher, The script is written, Undoing time

Do not attempt to figure out the events on the screen – the Spirit sees them all as the same. When the ego resists what is happening, there is only struggle and pain. As we begin to accept that the script is written, then we learn to open up to intimacy and love. Lynda is given a premonition of her husband dying and all of the days start to get confusing. It's not until she accepts what is happening and sees that it is all beyond her control that she starts to understand how everything works together. She then discovers the truth behind it all and learns to see "a miracle every day." The ego attempts to change or figure out what could be different, whereas through Spirit we learn that all things work together for good.

Priest (1994)

To live and attain the Life of Christ requires that all fears, guilt, shame, secrets, and hypocrisies be brought to the light of forgiveness. Truth must emerge in Its Simplicity as all lies are unveiled and released. Who can stand in judgment and be Innocent. And yet when all judgments are laid by, only Innocence remains! Christ leads us to the recognition of Eternal Love and to the Innocence and Beauty of Who we truly are.

Razor's Edge, The (1946 / 1984) Original and remake – Classic

The inward journey requires taking the Road less travelled. Relationships take on new meaning and any worldly goals formerly associated with them fall away as the new direction deepens. The desire to be truly helpful becomes the core of life, and in learning to be truly helpful we are Helped. Forgiveness, seeing past appearances to the love inside, is the key to happiness and Awakening. Those who follow the Spirit within march to the beat of a different drummer— One not of this world.

Reluctant Saint, The (1962)

"I do not know the thing I am, and therefore do not know what I am doing, where I am, or how to look upon the world or on myself. Yet in this learning is salvation born. And What you are will tell you of Itself." T-31.V.17

Only an open mind in a state of true humility can receive revelation from God. Jesus taught that you have to be as a little child to enter the Kingdom of Heaven. The scholarly *"I know mind"* is not only unnecessary to enter the Kingdom of Heaven, it bars the way. The presence of God abides where It is welcome, where there is a complete lack of judgment. When the final vestiges of self-doubt are washed from the mind, the world is transcended.

This is an inspiring film about the life of Joseph of Cupertino, who became known as a levitating saint. Joseph had no worldly skills or abilities and, in the eyes of his family and fellow friars, he failed at every worldly task assigned to him. Incapable of judgment or attaining worldly knowledge, Joseph was drawn to simplicity and opportunities to offer kindness and love. Along with his deep devotion to God, he offered his willingness to follow every instruction given to him by both the priests who doubted him and the priest who believed in him. By doing so, he experienced a transformation of consciousness that left him so unidentified with this world that he was often lifted up to float high above the earth.

Repeaters (2010)

Repeaters is an acute representation of how our only basis for decision making in the present is past regret, holding us hostage to the ego – set up again and again to replay the same story in an attempt to heal the same perceived hurts.

"Unless you learn that past pain is an illusion, you are choosing a future of illusions and losing the many opportunities you could find for release in the present." T-13.IV.6

In this movie three juvenile delinquents in a correction facility are given a day to "make amends." Each embarks on a genuine first step in facing their mistakes, yet the forgiveness the world offers makes error real and offers no escape from guilt. It is impossible to find peace by attempting to atone for perceived sins. As their day repeats the Spirit offers many opportunities to see that correction is in the mind.

It is the Forgiveness of their self-concepts that is required to free them – the good-brother-hero, the bad-son-rebel, and the victim-daughter "*face* of innocence." Mistaken in who they are, every action they take to alleviate guilt amplifies it instead, spiraling into the vicious chaos of "an eye for an eye." It is only when the miracle descends (the snow) that an out-of-pattern Holy Instant can return sanity, allowing us to see beyond the drama. We are always given another opportunity to repeat, to choose to accept the Atonement for ourselves and be released from what never was. The only question is: will it be today?

Revolver (2005)

Gambler, Jake Green is out of jail after seven years in solitary confinement, having taken the fall for his boss. Doing time has taken him inward; he has been shown *the game* and how to win it. He has one final lesson when he turns up in Vegas looking to exact revenge on his *perceived* enemy, the corrupt casino boss, Macha. Mr. Green still believes that "cash is king" and that having money and power is winning. The Spirit must reach us wherever we believe we are. This is the story of redemption through the exaggerated filter of gangster *respect* and *fear*. Here at a gross level can the game of human life truly be seen. Everything we do is motivated to maintain a facade, a self-concept. That is why we stay in terrible jobs or in bad relationships. We desire to be right about who we believe we are; we stay "for that slap on the back" that says that you are a good guy, a good gangster, a good father. "The greatest con that he [the ego] ever pulled was making you believe that he is you," that his thoughts and feelings are yours.

We do not always recognize our mighty companions when they show up; Avi and Zach teach Jake that he is still in prison and that it is his mind that needs to be freed from *the game*. In the truly practical application of the principles he has learned, they lead him through a series of assignments designed to flush the ego (Mr. Gold) fully into awareness. Mr. Green must give all to have all. And in a truly magnificent elevator scene he recognizes that the voice of fear is not his Real Identity. Now truly released in a state of Forgiveness, nothing can touch him.

Rigoletto (1993)

The "spell" of this world is believing in appearances and forgetting all the beauty inside. When the heart shuts down, an anger seems to grow in its place. But an opportunity arises to extend love and the heart begins to open again. And in forgiveness, looking past appearances entirely, we are reminded of the inner beauty that was always present. Fairy tales can come true; it can happen to you, when you are pure in heart. There is a song in all of us waiting to be sung. We need only let go of limitations and doubts and judgments for the song to come through.

Romeo and Juliet (1996) – Special relationship

Romantic love (the idea of bodies in love) carries with it the tragedy of all illusions. No illusion is what it seems to be. In a world where love is seen to be exclusive and dependent on bodies being together, relationships end. In such madness, the crazy idea of *union in death* seems to be the only hope there is. Here is the absurdity of the world made most apparent. True Union is no illusion, for It has Being in the Eternal One, God. Spiritual Union lasts forever. What transitory, ephemeral, fleeting experience of the world of bodies can last? "Nothing real can be threatened. Nothing unreal exists." (ACIM, intro.) Herein lies True Love.

Ruby Sparks (2012)

Manifesting can be a helpful steppingstone, but in the end you will learn to yield to the miraculous Flow of letting everything be Given. The mind is powerful and will always manifest what it believes and wants in any given moment, be it lack and loneliness or companionship and joyful interaction. The only thing you can control is the direction of your thinking. This is a path of being done *through*. Even if you think you can arrange the characters in a way that makes you happy, in the end–whether they do what you think you want or not–you will realize you have to let go of the ego's plan for salvation. Without the Spirit's Purpose, life is just a great distraction leading nowhere.

This is the lesson the main character Calvin learns when he sees that he needs to release the concept of "Ruby" to the Spirit. When he types, "When Ruby leaves the house, the past will be released," he frees himself from the ego's plan and opens his mind to the joy of the Holy Instant!

When the power of the mind is given over to Spirit in trust, seeming needs are met, including that of a relationship (if truly Helpful) and loving miracles start to occur naturally. Enjoy this sweet movie on instant manifestation of thought with a relationship theme!

Scarlet Letter, The (1995)

After all the finger-pointing, blaming, and scapegoating the ego offers, the Still, Small Voice for God gently reminds of Eternal Innocence. Who can say what "sin" is in the eyes of God? Let he who is without "sin" cast the first stone is another way of saying that the Innocent cannot judge or condemn. "Sin" is the illusion. Innocence is Reality. Love is Reality. Happy is the Child of God that knows Eternal Innocence and Perfection. Such is the Truth!

Searching for Debra Winger (2002) Documentary – Mind-watcher for self-concept

This documentary can be used to look at body thoughts and personal identity. It exposes the belief in womanhood and the actress self-concept. Here are two great quotes from the movie:
"Everyone that is not you, but is living with you, is a problem."
"Half of each is none of either."

Searching for Sugar Man (2012)

The Christ will never be recognized by the world. To the Christ presence, worldly recognition is irrelevant. The Spirit's message comes through the channels that are open, and the messages are simply for those with the ears to hear. There is no purpose for the world other than the healing of God's Son, and every miracle that is offered is received, whether the "external world" appears to reflect this immediately or not.

Hypothetical thinking is irrelevant and hypothetical questions have no answer. The script is written; it plays out as it does. Only personal interpretation and investment in worldly outcomes can make aspects of the script appear to be a success story or a tragedy. To the Christ it is all the same. Reality is unaffected by the playing out of what never was. Reality is beyond the script.

Rodriguez was a humble poet and musician whose songs reached the hearts and minds of those hungry for an experience beyond the status quo of the 1970's (namely apartheid and governmental oppression). Unknown to him he inspired thousands, if not millions, to open up to the idea that there is another way.

Serendipity (2001) – Classic for "You can't mess it up!"

Love is inevitable! You cannot mess things up ultimately, since all things work together for good. This is a story of miracles and miracles and miracles. The signs are everywhere, the spontaneity is flowing, the script is written, and the feeling is being carried in Joy! Though doubt thoughts may seem to cast their shadows for a time, there is a Destiny of Love that will not be denied.

Everyone who meets was meant to meet, and like the movies *Chances Are, Deja Vu, Only You, LA Story, Sleepless in Seattle* and *Still Breathing,* everything always leads to Love eventually. Why wait? Be open right Now! I love You forever and ever Beloved One. You are Pure Love.

Sessions, The (2012)

The Sessions is based on a true story about opening up to love and new, unexplored experiences. Mark O'Brien has complete muscle atrophy due to childhood polio; he cannot move his body at all. With tremendous willingness he is able to face his fears and open his heart to love and joining – with the gentle help of a sex therapist. Though the means are unconventional, Mark's willingness lights the way. Those around him respond to his genuine presence; they too begin to open their hearts to love. This is a lovely and heart-opening movie about joining, healing, and forgiveness.

Shall We Dance? (2004)

Routines and roles and daily habits can seem so fixed and set that it can seem impossible to allow for the new. Yet when the yearning of the heart stirs, we are given an opportunity to connect and enter the Dance of Life. It may start slowly, for the Way seems very new, but as we take each series of steps, we gain confidence in the new Direction. Our willingness and eagerness to learn carries us and, with persistence, is reflected in all that surrounds us. We must release the past to completely enter into the Dance. And when we release all doubts and fears that have haunted us, we are One with the Eternal Dance!

Shawshank Redemption, The (1994)

Never lose sight of your Innocence. Never give up the hope of freedom. Be determined and persistent in your goal to Awaken. Keep the fire of faith alive in your heart. For you shall reach Enlightenment. You must be Who You Are. Don't let an illusion of a journey depress you. Life is a present joy, and in laughter and happiness you Ascend!

Shutter Island (2010) – Mind-watcher for self-concept, Healing fearful thoughts and memories

A refusal to look upon the darkness and what the mind believes it has done leads to a fantasy world of complexity, confusion and sophisticated defense mechanisms. The belief in separation runs so deep that it constantly draws forth witnesses of victimization. Guilt and attack thoughts are projected onto characters and scenarios as a way of keeping them from awareness. Unconscious guilt is like a tape running in the mind, spinning stories as a defense against the truth.

While the world is willing to play out the fantasy, it is also ready to assist in the dismantling of the delusion under the care and Guidance of Spirit. Everyone is playing their assigned role and all it takes is a willingness to question every belief one holds. Admitting the guilt is a first step in healing. Forgiveness for what you believe you did (separate from God) will release. The world as you know it is made up. Through a fractured lens what is perceived through the body's eyes are witnesses to beliefs in the mind. Being willing to look upon the darkness is a step towards letting it go.

Simon Birch (1998)

This movie takes us through the spiritual journey, starting with the awareness of "something missing" (the father) and ending with the reunion. We witness the undoing of specialness, learning that there is no loss. This is the undoing of the idea that there ever was a separate individual doing anything. We gladly accept our True Innocence and bask in the amazing Love felt in the holy relationship between the two boys.

This movie is a beautiful opportunity to deepen in Faith. Being fully *who you are*, is what speaks; teaching is demonstrating. Simon teaches by accepting his function and stepping into it, no matter how stupid it seems in the eyes of the world. His uncompromising trust and deep devotion to playing his part in the Plan for Salvation is what shines on everyone; it is recognized by those who have an open heart.

You will see what you believe about yourself. When you come to know your Unshakable Innocence the whole world will be that reflection, even if it seems that people are "against" you. That is what Jesus taught with his prayer, "Forgive them, Father, for they know not what they do." He didn't see anything wrong; he didn't see a problem. It was all part of the Plan and could not be any other way.

The waltz of characters coming and going is part of the awakening process. A new character appears just as another one seems to disappear. We learn that Love is not in a person, but in the Self. Love goes on forever when it is not limited to anything or anyone specific. Consistency of Love comes from staying uncompromisingly aligned with Spirit. As the lessons are learned, the characters shift, leading to the inevitable reunion with the Father and the Wholeness that Is.

S1mOne (2002) – Classic for self-concept

Persona means mask. Personality is the mask of person-hood – the pretense of pretending to be a person, which is a covering over of the Reality of Spirit. What if person-hood was only a construct, a digital fabrication of images and memories that seemed to take on a life of their own? This movie exposes the construct of person-hood, the lie that masquerades as "life" in and of the body. The star of the dream is the hero of the dream, the body, the person, and in this movie, it is Simone. Simone is valued by the world for her beauty, her sex appeal, her fame, her skills, and her accomplishments. She is worshiped as if she were a God.

This is the story of the ego and the temptation to make and uphold a false construct for personal recognition. It is also a story that shows it is impossible to kill the ego, for death is what the ego belief is. Yet having been exposed, the ego's nothingness is apparent. "We're alright with fake, Dad, just don't lie about it" means that in order to forgive the construct it is important to not attempt to cover over, protect, or lie about the original error. This is a Call to take the lid off of all erroneous beliefs and release them. Christ Calls everyone. The world of bodies and persons is illusion, it is fake, now just don't lie about it. There is no need to protect or hide the ego belief that made the time-space cosmos and person-hood. Forgive, and know that "nothing real can be threatened, nothing unreal exists. Herein lies the peace of God." (ACIM, intro.) All Glory to the Living One that can never be simulated.

Sleepless in Seattle (1993)

Live by your heart's desire. Destiny will arrive, and bring all the joy alive in you. Clinging to a past memory obscures the opportunity for present joy. But beyond the "should" and "knowing" of the ego, the Spirit answers the Call for Help in wondrous ways: a son who never stops believing is used as an instrument for healing; a father's plea is broadcast across the country; a woman with other plans hears the call and despite doubts joins in the Answering. The script is written. When we listen to the Call within and follow, we experience the Joy intended for us all along!

Sliding Doors (1998) – Quantum awakening

You can Awaken "sooner" or Awaken "later." The choice is yours. This movie offers the insight that free will does not mean you can establish the curriculum, which is forgiveness and releasing past thoughts. Only the time you take it (grasp the lesson) is voluntary. Two scenarios are played out side by side, each initiated by a slight change in the event of attempting to catch a train ride home. In one scenario, deception is exposed immediately; in the other, the deception seems to linger and fester. Exposed deception can seem more traumatic at first, yet such exposure opens the door to healing much faster than when private thoughts and secrets are clung to and protected. Ask for an end to self-deception and watch the miracles spring forth at every turn of the script. Love waits on welcome, not on time. Be willing, for you are worthy.

Slumdog Millionaire (2008) – Illustrates the script is written and all things work together for the good

Jamal is doing well on India's *Who Wants to be a Millionaire* show, where the big question is A) Did he cheat? B) Is he lucky? C) Is he a genius? Or, D) Is everything destined? (That is, is it "written"?) The Spirit reveals that everything in Jamal's life was used for reconnecting with love (symbolized by his faithful friend Lakita). As he holds his goal out front, without getting distracted by trauma or success, he is able to finally accept that he does not know the answer to any of the world's riddles. He follows his heart and moves intuitively through life. In this trust and willingness to not know, everything is given to him as he marvels that the answer is D) The script is written. It is only a change of purpose – seeing that form is of the past – that can solve all problems now.

Snow Walker (2003) – Holy relationship

A man in the wilds of Canada begrudgingly offers help to a sick Eskimo girl. But after a plane accident, he is forced to accept her help so that they can join together and find their way home. Who is in need of healing? Pride and autonomy are flushed into awareness for healing so that true humility can be experienced. Holy relationship is between the Father and Son. Yet as a means to experience this, we are given relationships in this world where separate interests are laid aside to experience a shared goal. All abilities are given over to serve the whole, and a holy relationship is born. They are each the other's savior.

Solaris (2002) – Classic, Metaphysical

A journey to the experience of complete forgiveness. Past associations are thoughts which keep returning to awareness until it dawns that "I remembered her wrong." People represent incompletion and death until they are forgiven, and in forgiveness only the Joy and

Love remain. Though in fear there can be an attempt to cast away unhealed thoughts, they return until they can be seen in forgiveness and thus truly released. The journey can seem startling as these past thoughts return to awareness, yet they represent only what the ego made of them. As they are released they are seen anew and everything is forgiven.

Someone to Love (1987)

Gathered in a theater that is about come down, the search for love and meaning in this world is documented. Participants receive an invitation to come to a party, and those that show up are interviewed about all aspects of the search for "someone to love." Like the movie *Breaking Up*, this movie shows the frustration, confusion and despair of looking for love outside One Self. Expectations are never met by any "body" and in the end there is no way of explaining the search for meaning in the meaningless. Intimacy and meaning are within, and nothing is outside One Self.

Something's Gotta Give (2003) – Classic for relationship

This is a sparkling movie gem of healing and forgiveness, a glorious movie of character transformation! The past, with all its guilt, insecurities, fear of intimacy and pride, has *gotta give* way to Love. And it does! Love has nothing to do with age and nothing to do with time. It is all about the willingness to open up the heart and take a chance on expressing the total depth there. The past seems to be in your face when you are willing to experience Love, and past thought patterns cannot be ignored or pushed down in awareness when there is a true desire to connect. It seems like a big leap, a bold step of faith, but the rewards for taking this leap are Pure Love, Happiness, and Joy! The stress of clinging to the ego gives way and in the Joy of Love, True Giving from the heart is restored. Such a great parable of forgiveness!

Somewhere in Time (1980)

With the unified power of desire, time cannot keep us from a Union of Love. Love transcends the belief in time and distance as we journey back to the Beginning: Life in and as Love. There is a Perspective in which time and space are under the direction of miracles and all is seen through forgiving eyes. In this Perspective it is apparent that we have never been apart. Time cannot veil the True Union and the True Eternal Love!

Source Code (2011)

We all accept the reality we are presented with. Captain Colter Stevens awakens to the call of Goodwin who initiates a recall sequence orientating him to the self-concept of an air force pilot trained to obey. Yet as he attempts to follow through on his mission he begins to question his purpose. Patched into the last eight minutes of the consciousness of Sean, a school teacher on an exploding Chicago-bound train, Captain Stevens must initiate an investigation to find the bomber and foil his next target. This is an exercise in time, space and the willingness to follow beyond our present understanding. Yet as the second bomb plot unravels so does the Captain's perception of the world. Launched into this repeat sequence of peak awareness he must question the very nature of his reality. His identity begins to soften as he interacts with Christina, a mighty companion who draws his attention out of the drama and into a present moment intimacy beyond his methodical role.

The belief in loyalty and duty of care is questioned in this intensely distractive mission. Can Captain Colter Stevens honor his country *and* the deeper call of his heart? Reciprocity, compromise and people pleasing are all highlighted in this story. The captain must find a way to transcend his limiting beliefs and desire to be a good soldier, to rise in pure faith into an entirely new existence. Forgiveness is the release; having made peace with his Father he is relieved of duty, free to live an unexpected and loving life.

Sphere (1998) – The power of thought

The world was made so that the power of Divine Mind could be forgotten. Meaningless thoughts of fear show a meaningless world of fear. The world is an invention of false thought, and is thus only an attempt to misuse the Power of Mind. As the mind's power is revealed, the next step is to realize that this world is simply a projection of attack thoughts and that these thoughts can have no real effect since they have no real source. The Real Alternative is to forgive and release all attack thoughts. This Alternative can only be chosen when the mind is ready to remember Self as Spirit at One with God, in Whom all True Power resides. The "decision to forget" must be raised to awareness so that the Real Alternative, the final decision, "the decision to remember God," can be made at last.

Spiderman 3 (2007)

It is not until we allow all dark thoughts to fully surface and be healed that we can know who we are, consistently. Otherwise deep rooted grievances and misperceptions will cling to us like a sticky rubber suit, and will seem to run our lives. Even Spiderman must heal his past associations in order to be truly helpful. We must see that we remembered our brother wrong, and no-one, not even our self, is guilty. Our worthiness is remembered and Purpose is given when we wish to see our brother sinless. Then we can join with our friends in innocence.

Spirit: Stallion of the Cimarron (2002) Animated – Classic for authority problem and rebellion, Metaphysical

Where there once was autonomy and defiance – through trust, willingness and gentleness it is seen that the Spirit's way is the way to freedom. At first it is interpreted as sacrifice and loss of control, but eventually it is seen that there are blessings in accepting Spirit's call – which is our own. Rebellion leads to continued struggle, but surrender opens up to friendship and brotherhood. Surrender leads back to the lands where we are joined with the mighty wings of an eagle.

Star Trek: First Contact (1996)

As the Borg "assimilate" beings to build an ever-expanding collective identity, so the Federation values independence and freedom of individuals to choose and preserve a personal identity. Both concepts (personal identity and collective identity) assume the existence of private mind, and as such are nothing but make-believe illusions. Divine Mind is Singular and Unified and there is no other. All is One in the Mind of God, and only this Mind is Real.

Star Trek: Insurrection (1998)

At last the purpose of "space travel" is questioned: "Where is there to go?" The inward journey of exploration stands in stark contrast to exploring the galaxies of the cosmos. The values of simplicity, defenselessness, and innocence are placed before technology and conquest. Something is Greater than the needs of the "many" or the needs of the "few" or the Prime Directive: It is Truth. The value of approaching the present moment, when time slows and everything is experienced fully in Stillness, is a sign that Awakening from the dream of the world is close at hand. What time but now can truth be known?

Still Breathing (1997) – Classic for worthiness of love

The belief in unworthiness and the belief in a cold, heartless, random world are one and the same. The faith in miracles, the spark of joy, visions, intuitions, and loving tenderness are one and the same. This is a love story about a man who believed in finding true love, and a woman who came to believe. It is an uplifting reminder to never give up hope on the deepest desire of your heart, to know and be known, to love and be loved. Dreams of childhood innocence reflect the Divine Innocence within, and miracles bring this Innocence back into awareness. Beneath the hard, cold persona lies the heart of an angel, waiting to be discovered. Ask and you shall be Given, knock and the door shall be opened. There is a destiny that makes us One. None goes their way alone. All that we send into the lives of others comes back into our own. We are the same One, and this is realized in a moment of forgiveness. All differences are gone at last. You are worthy of Love My Beloved. So very worthy.

Tangled (2010) – Trusting intuition, Healing perception, Undoing self-concepts and special relationships

Let your hair down and escape the prison you have made! If you have the courage to follow your heart, the Spirit will send in characters to help break you free from this world. People pleasing, or in this case mother pleasing, holds the main character back from her Calling. Rapunzel has been living a lie. She must learn to see that she has projected her fear onto her mother and then take her steps regardless of outcome. She feels an inner calling to extend, shine, explore and join, yet the voice of the ego warns her against ever venturing outside of her ivory tower.

Year after year she is prompted to find out why thousands of lit lanterns fly up into the night sky, intuitively aware there is a deeper meaning that could reveal her true identity. When she makes the leap of faith, unlikely mighty companions show up to help her to face issues of trust, abandonment, and the undoing of the mother-daughter concept. Her desire to experience life, to know the truth, and to open her heart to love inspires those around her to get in touch with their own hearts' desire.

Ten Commandments, The (1956)

Be faithful unto the Lord Thy God. Hold no idols or graven images before Him. For God has offered a way back to Eternal Love. Be faithful to God's Law of Love. The story of Moses is a parable of turning your life over to God and following His sure direction. The sea of duality cannot prevent you from remembering Eternal Oneness. Have faith and you shall be lead to the promised Oneness, for that is What You Are in Truth!

Thaw, The (1996) TV Series, Star Trek Voyager, Season 2, Episode 23 – Metaphysical

Asleep and dreaming in a self-imposed, computer-controlled hibernation, an entire world is generated from the emotion of fear. There seems to be no escape for the hostages from the bizarre world of masks and games and costumes and characters. Fear seems to be in complete control. Those who chose to sleep seem to have given their power over to fear, which it uses to perpetuate itself and all the sets and characters it has made up. To bring about release, attempts are made to "reason with," "negotiate with," "bargain with," and "compromise with" fear. They fail. Yet in the end it is discovered that fear must be directly faced and exposed as the nothingness it is before there can be release and true freedom. It is time to Wake Up!

Thérèsè: The Story of Therese of Lisieux (2004) – Miracles, magic, and prayer

Her Love for God and her simple discovery that holiness can be achieved by small acts of love and compassion became Therese's spiritual path, which became known as the Little Way. It was Therese's simplicity and gentleness that inspired Mother Theresa to take her name and adopt the Little Way as her own. Although the belief in sacrifice is prevalent throughout this film, it is worth watching. The simple lesson that Therese learns and teaches is that you cannot prove your worth through "doing." Loving God and being who you are is the only gift that you have to give – and it is enough.

Thirteenth Floor, The (1999) – Classic, Metaphysical

This film provides another great opportunity to see beyond the "virtual reality" made up by the ego. In seeming realm after realm, the images and characters seem to be very real, yet they but represent the inventions, wishes, and desires of the ego acted out in form. As it dawns in awareness that none of the scenarios are real, this realization beckons the question: Then what is the point? Suddenly, the forgiven world appears! Forgiveness of illusions is the point! In forgiveness there is only the happy dream of non-judgment. And the world is lit and shining in the light of our Source. Only a blessing remains, where once there seemed to be a threat. All pain is over now. Only love is reflected in the forgiven world. How blessed is the world when it has been forgiven. Nightmares are gone from awareness, and it is clear that they never were at all.

Three Wishes (1995)

The only lesson to learn about this world is complete gratitude and appreciation for everything and everyone AS IS. This is the giving up of the belief in hypothetical thinking (that things could be or would have been better off if they were different). Truly all things work together for good and this is experienced from the Spirit's Perspective (Now), which is high above and far beyond all personal judgments, classifications and expectations. Situational wishes often seem to be granted, but the Grandest Wish of All is forgiveness, reflecting the All-Inclusiveness of Love. What greater gift could there be than to look on all things with great love, gratitude, and full appreciation (a forgiven world) and to Awaken to the Eternal Love of God.

Time Traveler's Wife, The (2009) – Classic, Relationship

A rare movie that beautifully shows that love is beyond time. The main character is moving through time, and experiences different parts of his life centered around a relationship. The partnership in this movie is one in which expectations are constantly being undone. To the ego, it is jolting when a partner keeps disappearing, and in this movie it can happen at any moment. Any sense of desiring a "normal (special) relationship" leads to disappointment. The only way to look upon it all is from the perspective of opening up to a Love that transcends time, space, and bodies entirely.

Titanic (1997) – Love

As the ship of the world (fame, fortune, pleasure, status, recognition, speed, and a glittering diamond) sinks to the depths of its own darkness, I know that the true Heart of the Ocean (Love) rises and goes on and on. Thank you, Spirit, for the recognition of What is Real and Valuable and Meaningful. Once more You open the Door; You are here in My Heart and My Heart does go on and on. Love is the saving Grace. Though the ways of the world once seemed to suffocate and imprison, living in the faith of the moment has brought a freedom that reaches to Eternity. Thank You God! You are Here. There is nothing I fear, 'cause I know that My Heart does go on and on.... Love is Everlasting!

Total Recall (1990)

Virtual reality is an artificial environment that seems completely real. One can "program" the scene as one wishes it to be. Such is the world. Based on the belief that you can author yourself and your world to a particular preference or liking, the wish seems to manifest. Yet how can a wish to be something You are not, succeed? In dreams it may seem to succeed, but not in Reality. A journey away from the One Self is a fantasy, and therefore cannot occur. God is the Author of Reality. This is the Fact to be accepted. How joyful is the realization that there is no Love but God's and that there is no life, mind, intelligence, or substance in matter. Remembrance of God is the only True Experience of *Total Recall*.

Truman Show, The (1998) – Classic, Metaphysical, The world is in the mind

This is a fantastic awakening movie about the undoing, and having the courage to follow the call of the heart. The world was a show produced and directed by the ego. It employed many actors, used many sets and events on a time loop, and depended on sales, labels, and product placement to sustain itself. The show aimed at drama, repetitions, distractions, pretense, and ultimately resorted to fear to perpetuate itself, for being make-believe it had to be believed as real to seem to continue. Once the show is seen as nothing but a contrived skit of past memories, the show no longer seems to be Reality. Once you see the show from the fearless Perspective, the show is effectively over and done, for fear has been exposed as unreal, and all the characters and sets are therefore without meaning. You are the light of the world and no longer a character on the screen. Who you are (Spirit) is the meaning of Life! Our Kingdom is not of this world!

Two Girls and a Guy (1997) – Special relationship

This movie is a raw, direct exposure of the ego's tactics of denial and projection. It is an uncovering of the deceptions, defenses, and diversions of the ego in its attempts to cover its tracks and stay hidden. True Love does not possess. True Love has nothing to hide. Yet in worldly "personal relationships," the desire to possess remains unforgiven, for all such relationships are constructed by the ego. Along with the concept of personal relationships comes envy, jealousy, rage, lust, guilt, shame, betrayal, rejection, abandonment, distrust, and a variety of forms of fear. The ego's theme song is *You don't know me,* but the Spirit's theme song is I AM THAT I AM. Glory be to God for Our Real Relationship in Spirit!

Ultimate Gift, The (2006) – Classic, Guidance

Our Father wills to give us everything, but it is only through mind training and maturing in the Spirit that His Gifts can be recognized and accepted. Obeying the Spirit leads to the acceptance of the Ultimate Gift (the Atonement). Jason has lived a shallow and unfulfilled life of material luxury but as a condition of his grandfather's will, he is presented with the opportunity to receive a series of Gifts, leading to the Ultimate Gift. These prompts, and the opportunity to obey and follow, are the Spirit's way of leading the mind to seeing that what was thought of as sacrifice actually leads to a blessing.

In this world we cannot tell our advances from our retreats. It is only the experience of peace that is our barometer. What the mind previously valued can be let go of and replaced with values of the Spirit–integrity, friendship, and laughter. Intuitive ability is heightened and a sense of service is experienced through the washing away of egoic patterns and desires. A new state of mind is realized and all things of the world naturally become meaningless. The ultimate gift is ordinary; it is just the recognition of who you are.

Uncorked – At Sachem Farm (1998) – Self-concept

This movie shows the way the Spirit can work with the mind that believes salvation lies in ambition and success. It is a movie about opening up and accepting one's function. Ross is an entrepreneur who has lost his way both financially and spiritually. He comes to realize that he has been avoiding his Calling and hiding behind the pretense of being the "responsible one" of the family. The Spirit comes through Uncle Cullen in unexpected ways, setting into motion events that change the lives of everyone in the family. On the spiritual journey, there can be many distractions and temptations that try to lead the mind astray from one's true calling. The world is a huge distractive device; what is going on is a never-ending and unceasing denial of Purpose and Truth. The way out is a change of mind, an acceptance of the Purpose of Forgiveness, and the recognition that there is nothing out there to try and nothing to be done before accepting the always-present Function to share the simple joy of saying Yes to the Identity as Spirit!

Vanilla Sky (2001) – Classic, The power of thought

Virtual "reality" seems so real that the line between imagination, fantasy and the stories of the world can seem blurred. Similarly, the line between nighttime dreams and daily living can seem blurred. What if you were unaware that you were dreaming? What if the dream reflected only your own unconscious wishes, desires, and whims? And what if you had the power to allow the nightmares to be released and to dream a happy dream of non-judgment instead? There is a leap of faith required in laying aside all attempts to control the dream. Yet in the leap there is bliss, for the dream is Given back anew from the Spirit. The world will end in Joy because it was a place of sadness. The world will end in laughter for it was a place of sorrow. A happy dream is Given you, to take the place of all nightmares that seemed to haunt your holy mind. Welcome to the real world, Beloved child of God. Welcome Home!

Venice, Venice (1992)

What is real and what is illusion? Are making a movie, being a character in a movie, or experiencing this world from a personal perspective really any different? What constitutes acting and being an actor as contrasted with being authentic and being real "in this world?" From the world's perspective there is a distinction made between "real life" human dramas and "the movies." From the Spirit's Perspective, however, there is no such distinction. All is One. Everything is connected. Life is a State of Mind, a State of Being, and is far beyond error (the world of bodies and events and dramas and scenarios). God is the only Cause. Truth is true and only the truth is true!

Village, The (2004) – Metaphysical mind-watcher, Spiritual community, Distorted perception

A seemingly tranquil village has a dark secret that the elders do not want revealed. The only way to keep a secret is through deception and masks. Nothing is as it seems. There is nothing to fear but our own made up prisons that keep us in the illusion of safety. Security lies not in special groups or safe communities but in unlocking the box of secrets to see their nothingness. There is no need for deception or fear. On the Spirit-led path to Innocence there is no need for creating "those we do not speak of." Trust your calling; let Innocence can lead the way. There is no need for magic. Simple faith and trust are all that is required.

Waking Life (2001) Animated

This is an animated exploration of the ambiguity of dreaming and the desire for the ultimate release of Awakening. When it becomes apparent that it is impossible to figure out the dream, the option of Waking Life begins to dawn. It seems as though there are many moments in history, yet each instant is merely a refusal of God that seems to perpetuate in time. *Waking* is simply saying "Yes!" to God now. "Yes" is the end of conflict that sprang from the "no."

Whale Rider (2002)

No matter the circumstances, your Call for God will be answered. The situation you believe prevents you from being with God is actually your training ground, the very situation to Forgive – your way out.

"The last shall be the first and the first shall be last." (Matthew 20:16) The ego can try to disguise itself with talk about truth, like the seeming leader in this movie, but it does not want to see that truth is Given.

What about Bob? (1991)

Who is the therapist and who is the patient? Who is the Healer? The personal perspective cannot heal because it is the very definition of sickness. The Spirit's Perspective is Healing for It is of the Spirit, the only Healer. The ego's pretense of "personal healing" is exposed as a farce in this comedy about the "unhealed healer." All anger comes from guilt, and all guilt comes from holding onto a personal self-image or personal perspective on the world. The world of fragmentation and the personal self are two aspects of the same illusion – the personal perspective. How glorious is the Oneness which God created Perfect and Eternal! How magnificent the Self which God created in His Own Likeness of Spirit and Light! True Healing is the Gateway to the remembrance of God.

What Dreams May Come (1998) – Special relationship

The world is the pictorial representation of false thought, much like the canvas represents the painter's foolish imaginings. The world is nothing more than what sleepiness and forgetfulness dreams it to be. Change your mind about the dream entirely and you will see the world differently. There is no "life" or "afterlife" or "prior life," for all dreams are imagination. Yet the Spirit's temporary Purpose for dreams and images is to teach forgiveness – a unified Perspective. This Perspective is reached through the willingness to join. Despite all fears and doubts and warnings, be willing to join, to overlook illusions, and to recognize the One Self that is Love. Be so willing to join that you will journey through the darkness to the Light, through the hell of error to the Joy of Truth! We shall see with Vision when there is no fear to See what imagination was made to deny. Do not be afraid to look on the Love Within. Only the anticipation will frighten you. Come with open arms and lay down all defenses. God loves You forever!

What The Bleep Do We Know? (2004) – Classic, Quantum awakening

This movie shows that everything is connected, everything is thought. Everything you perceive is the result of your thoughts. Amanda goes from frustration to realizing that it is her thoughts that are producing the entire world she perceives. Once you realize this you are no longer at the mercy of the world. You can find happiness within your own heart because you are not dependent on the world; it is dependent on you. When you change your mind and come to the present moment, you have dominion over the images. You can still your mind and achieve peace of mind and lasting happiness.

You have to understand the power of your beliefs and your thoughts. Quantum scientists are beginning to wake up and see the power of the mind, but are still confusing the brain with the mind. Neurotransmitters and peptides are the same as thoughts because thoughts make up everything. The scientists say that you create reality by making your own perceptions. Perceptions are temporary, unlike God and Eternity. The scientists say you make your future, your past, and the world, but the world is an invention, a fabrication, a fiction; it will disappear. It is just a learning device that Spirit uses to teach you to forgive and to see the power of your mind. The scientists say we are all one; we are all connected. When you forgive the world, you see the world as in your mind. As scientist Fred Alan Wolf states, "There is no 'out there' out there."

What the Bleep? Down the Rabbit Hole (2006) – Classic, Quantum awakening

As you watch these movies, let the Spirit remind you of the Purpose. The Spirit will constantly remind you, "Do not try to figure any of it out. Pull your mind into the abstract. There is no objective world out there and you cannot separate the observed from the observer."

What Women Want (2000) – No private thoughts

Nick is a self-centered marketing manager who thinks he's God's gift to women. He is shocked to find that he can hear women's thoughts. At first this physic ability is frightening to accept. He attempts to use his newly discovered ability for personal gain but as he begins to pay closer attention to what he hears he realizes how blind he has been to the relationships in his life. Opportunities to be helpful arise and his final lesson is one of integrity, in which a decision has to be made to end the deception, making room for an authentic relationship.

When a Man Loves a Woman (1994) – Special relationship

In this film, we find that what looks like a happy couple who has "everything going for them" is actually a cover for desperation and fear. This needs to come up and be exposed. The movie beautifully lays out a practical demonstration of a movement into greater honesty. Being willing to expose everything that is believed, without hiding, is an essential step. That is what partners are for – to be a mirror for each other in order to clear away the darkened glass through which the mind looks.

Although there may be separation, new friends, and even drama, the Holy Spirit uses it all for the healing of the mind. It takes great trust to not try to fix anything and just be honest. Although true honesty is a consistent state of mind, it is essential to be honest about one's emotions to come to this state. As Jesus says in the Course, the one right use of judgment is "How do I feel?" This is the barometer with which to see if I am in alignment with the Spirit or not.

When Harry Met Sally (1989)

Relationship, when opened to healing, leads to Love. The ego sought the relationship to fill a need and find "completion" in a partner. The Spirit flushes up the desire to be separate and autonomous and all the perceived differences and "lacks" of the ego perspective. Completion cannot be found outside, for Love is within. True Love dawns as perceived differences are transcended and grievances are all released. It is possible to share a Purpose that leads to the experience of Love. It is possible to experience Love's Magnitude as littleness and unworthiness are gently, voluntarily laid aside.

Wide Awake (1998)

A child named Joshua begins to question the meaning of life after his beloved grandfather dies. He asks for a sign from God and despairs that he has not been heard. Yet in the end he realizes that an angel has been with him amongst his classmates all along. The signs of the Spirit are as near and clear as we are ready and willing to see and hear. God always Answers the prayer of the Heart! The Lord is my shepherd; I shall not want ... He leadeth me beside the still waters ... He restoreth my soul ... Yea, though I walk through the valley of the shadow of death, I will fear no evil, for Thou art with me ... Surely goodness and mercy shall follow me all the days of my life, and I will dwell in the house of the Lord forever. Amen.

Wizard of Oz, The (1939) – Classic, Metaphysical

The world is like a dream, at times it even seems like a nightmare. When you forget you are dreaming, everything feels so real. Yet deep inside you are aware that you are simply lost, looking to get back Home. In the dream it seems as if you are a body meeting other bodies along the way. There are pains and there are pleasures but eventually they are all seen as the same. With this awareness comes total disillusionment with the dream. This leaves room for the miracle! Filled with gratitude and love you learn that you always had the power to go home. You had mistakenly been looking outside your Self for it. Verily I say, it is your desire for God that will Awaken you to your Eternal Home. Close your eyes, relax, and repeat after me: "There's no place like Home. There's no place like Home. There's no place like Home."

X-men (2000) – Classic for psychic phenomenon

All abilities can be used under Spirit's direction, in Purpose. If abilities are feared or used for control, then pain and destruction are inevitable. However, with love and patience, all seeming gifts, talents, or physic abilities can be used to remember our Divine Self, which is beyond all gifts and worldly phenomena.

Yentl (1983)

The desire to know God will take us all the way Home. Nothing is impossible! There is always a way to continue to follow our Calling, regardless of the ego's rules and boundaries. The longer our True Identity is kept hidden, the more elaborate the cover-up seems to be. Yet a moment comes when hiding Who we are and holding back our love is no longer possible – the desire for God is simply too strong! The decision to risk it all for God seems to be made over and over again as each step is taken. Letting go of the past allows everything to fall into its correct perspective. It served beautifully. The love of our life was always God. Papa, watch me fly!

Yes Man (2008)

This hilarious comedy is a classic for the symbol of stepping stones. Carl is repressed in all areas of his life. He has fallen into patterns of avoidance and isolation, saying no to just about everything. Through a series of events he is given a clear directive to say "yes" to every opportunity presented to him. Though at first he is fearful and resistant, the Spirit shows him that he really does not know his own best interests. Before long he is experiencing the joy of the miracle from following his prompt. His world opens up in wonderful ways and then, as happens with all stepping stones, this prompt is maximized and it becomes time for a deepening in discernment.

You Can't Take It with You (1938) – Classic

A beautiful story of the contrast between following the ways of the Spirit and the ego. The Spirit is steadfast and gently reminds that everything will work out great, while the ego frets about its goals of status, money, power, and control. The Spirit is symbolized by this open and free flowing house of Love. This movie is a very helpful tool for learning to discern the Voice for God that leads to the Kingdom of Heaven within. Such Joy!

Using Movies on the Inner Journey

In this Guide to Enlightenment movies that are helpful in awakening to Truth are re-viewed through the lens of True Forgiveness. Forgiveness is the complete laying aside of the ego – the belief in linear time/space. There is a way to watch movies that leads to the observation of events, scenes and scripts of the world with forgiving eyes. In this experience, forgiveness is synonymous with peace of mind and non-judgment.

Movies can be used to expand consciousness and, ultimately, experience the depth and meaning of the Inner Self. They can be a means for getting in touch with and releasing limiting beliefs, resulting in the resolution of inner conflict.

For those who have the ears to hear and eyes to see, movies are modern-day parables that offer a backdrop for experiencing deepening awareness and purpose – the detached, fearless Perspective from which it is apparent that "all things work together for good." Use them to uncover the Innocence and Beauty that is the Real Self as God created It.

Watch movies with a desire to let them be used by the Spirit to release the concepts of "past" and "future." Watch them with an earnest desire for deeper understanding and meaning. Your intention is not to repress the emotions you experience as you watch, but to release all unconscious beliefs and interpretations which prevent the constant experience of Peace and Joy. In releasing everything which does not serve you are transformed!

On the following page you will find David Hoffmeister's *Instrument for Peace*, a helpful tool for tracing upsets and emotions back to the mind.

Instrument for Peace

A practical guide for working through upsets and healing the mind

The mind at peace is healed. The mind at peace has whole-heartedly welcomed peace. In this world, lack of peace appears in many forms. For permanent healing to occur, lack of peace must be traced back to its singular cause in the mind. Use of this instrument for that tracing back can help a willing mind let go of what it thinks it knows, see the world differently, and experience a present state of peace and joy.

[NOTE: See page 103 for some helpful tips on each step.]

A = Past or future action, situation, or event
B = Upsetting emotions
C = Name and/or future consequence
D = My belief in lack (taking the form of an image of self/other/ the world)
E = Wanted and expected action, situation, or event

1. When I think about **A**: _____
    _____, I feel **B**: _____
    _____ because I think that
    C: _____ is to blame and/or
    I'm afraid that **C**: _____
    will occur in the future.

    [NOTE: What is your ego's perception of this? Write down the first things that come to your mind regarding **A**, **B**, and **C**.]

2. **A**, **B**, and **C** prove that I am right about **D**: _____
    _____.

    I do not like how I feel now, so I am ready to consider the possibility that the way I am perceiving this is not the way it really is. As part of the healing process, I am willing to look beyond my perception of this upset (the meaning I have given it) and look within my mind.

3. I want to learn that there is a way that I can, without guilt, see the part I play in thinking **A**: _____,
    in feeling **B**: _____
    in blaming **C**: _____, or in fearing
    C: _____.

4. I release my wanting to be right about my perception of **A**, **B**, **C**, and **D**. I want instead to be happy. Through the ego (distorted thinking/seeing), I perceive the cause of my upset and its resolution as outside my mind. This projection seems very real; its purpose is to distract my mind from looking inward.

5. If the cause of my upset and its resolution were outside my mind, I would, in fact, be powerless to change it. My use of projection (seeing outside what I don't want to see within) is why I seem powerless, why **C**: _____
    _____seem(s) to be the cause of my upset.

6. Thinking **A**: _____,
    feeling **B**: _____
    blaming **C**: _____, or in fearing
    C: _____ result
    from my belief in D: _____
    _____.

7. I am only upset at someone or something when they/it mirror(s) back to my mind a belief which I have denied from awareness. When I blame/fear something in the world, it is to avoid seeing the upset and resolution as they really are (a decision in my mind) and to instead maintain an image of self/other/the world as I wish. This mind trick seems to displace guilt and fear, but actually maintains feelings of upset. To blame or fear an image of self/other/the world requires that I believe I am limited to a body and world of bodies and denies the spiritual abstract reality of my being. As a first step in letting go of all upset, I want to see in my mind what I thought was outside it. Being upset about **A**: _____

is only another attempt to make **C:** _____
_____ the cause of my guilt and fear.

8. Upset seems valuable and justifiable when **A** runs counter to what I wanted. What I wanted and expected is **E:** _____
_____.

   I still believe in **D:** _____
   so I think I need **E:** _____
   _____ to be happy, complete, and at peace. Is this belief in lack, and the resulting expectation, more important to me than peace of mind?

9. Everything in the world works together for my good. What I think is the cause of my upset is not the cause at all. The choice to be upset is a choice not to see the cause, my belief in separation/lack, as a present decision in my mind. It's an attempt to see the cause in the past/future and the present as its effect.

10. What I want RIGHT NOW, above all else, is peace. I question my belief in **D:** _____ and I voluntarily let go of **E:** _____ in order to reconnect with my one goal: peace.

11. Peace of mind is a present decision which I gratefully choose RIGHT NOW! Guilt, and fear of consequences, only seemed possible because I was determined to hold on to a belief in past/future cause. I let go of the meaning I gave to the past/future and open my mind to the present. I am absolved and innocent.

12. I am grateful for the realization that the cause of my upset, which I thought was in the world, was actually only an unquestioned belief and decision in my mind. I have decided anew for my PEACE OF MIND.

Tips on the use of
the Instrument for Peace

"Lack of peace must be traced back to its singular cause in the mind." The singular cause is your mind's decision for the ego at the instant of separation, from which arises all your various "lack" beliefs. But don't get ahead of yourself and just write that in. Do your own tracing back, step by step. For it to be effective, be completely honest with yourself as you use this Instrument.

1. What is your ego's perception of this? Write down the first things that come to your mind regarding **A**, **B**, and **C**.

2. "**A**, **B**, and **C** prove *[to me]* that I am right about **D**"... look within my mind. *[at my beliefs]*

3. It is OK to adapt or refine your thoughts as you go along.

4. Read and contemplate.

5. Read and contemplate.

6. Think about **D**. What is the nature of your belief in lack that might be behind **A**, **B**, and **C**? Lack of control? Vulnerability? Lack of a certain quality in yourself? Body identification? Linear time?

7. Step 7 clarifies the nature of your projection.

8. In step 8, you do not need to be realistic about **E**. If you had a magic wand and could change anything, what would you ideally have wanted or expected?

9. In step 9, the Instrument addresses the higher mind, "and the present *[upset, your present state of mind]* as its effect."

10. "I voluntarily let go of **E** *[your hope to change a person or the world]* to reconnect with my one goal: peace *[of mind, joy]*"

11. All the images are false. None of it ever was. Nothing in the past is real or true.

12. I am the Son of God: free, whole and happy!

"The cause of my upset was only an unquestioned belief and decision in my mind." *[**D**, which you may reflect on and trace back even further, are you a person or spirit?]*

NOTES

NOTES

Index, Movies A – Z

Also by David Hoffmeister

Going Deeper
Only One Mind
Healing in Mind
Purpose is the Only Choice
Awakening through A Course in Miracles
My Meaning in Scripture

David's writings are available in print and ebook formats.
Select materials have been translated into Spanish, French,
Swedish, Chinese, Norwegian and Dutch.

Online Materials

www.livingmiraclescenter.org
www.awakening-mind.org
www.acim.me
www.acim.cc

Bibliography

A Course in Miracles, second ed.
Foundation for Inner Peace,
Mill Valley, CA 1996

Reference Abbreviations
T : Text
M : Manual for Teachers
W : Workbook for Students